A 2024 Starter Guide

Dresden, Germany

And Highlights of The Saxony Region

Barry Sanders – writing as:

B G Preston

Dresden, Germany

Copyright © 2024 by B G Preston / Barry Sanders

All rights reserved. No part of this book may be reproduced or transmitted in any form or by any means without written permission from the author via his Facebook page or cincy3@gmail.com. The author's Facebook page may be found at: www.Facebook.com/BGPreston.author. Comments on this work and others are invited.

ISBN: 9798876414960

1st edition – Updated May 2024- AR

Acknowledgements: The author greatly appreciates Sandra Sanders' contributions and guidance.

Photography: Maps and photos in the Starting-Point Guides are a mix of those taken by the author, Adobe Media, Shutterstock, Wikimedia, and Google maps. No photograph or map in this work should be used without checking with the author first. [1]

---

[1] This art, which is used throughout this guide, is the Dresden Coat of Arms.

Forward and Some Notes from the Author on the Starting-Point Guides Approach and Coverage.

What we look for in a travel guidebook can vary by each individual. Some travelers want great details into the history of every monument or museum, others may want details on area restaurants. This guide's coverage is a bit broader in approach. The goal of every Starting-Point Guide is to help orient you to the city and area, gain an understanding of its layout, how to get around, highlights of the town's treasures, and what is nearby.

Overviews are provided on the town, suggested lodging, points-of-interest, travel, and the area. A moderate level of detail is provided on restaurants, shops, museums, and other points of interest.

The end goal is for you to come away from your visit having a good understanding of what is here, what the town is like and not feeling that you have missed out on leading sights and attractions.

Happy Travels, *B G Preston*

Chapters & Contents

Preface 6
1: Dresden – The Capital of Saxony 13
2: When to Visit 28
3: Traveling to Dresden 34
4: Old Town Points of Interest 40
5: New Town Points of Interest 67
6: Attractions A Bit Further Out 75
7: Getting Around in Dresden...88
8: City & Area Passes and Tours..94
9: Where to Stay in Dresden 99
10: Day Trips from Dresden 106
Appendix: Helpful Online References 125
Index 131
Starting-Point Travel Guides 133

Dresden's Old Town / Altstadt

Preface
Area Covered & Some Suggestions

This Starting-Point Guide is intended for travelers who wish to really get to know a city and area and not just make it one quick stop on a tour through Germany or Europe[2]. Oriented around the

Zwinger Palace in Old Town / Altstadt
Photo source: Wikipedia

---

[2] **One Day Itinerary:** While the focus of this guide is using Dresden as a basecamp for several days, the author realizes that many visitors will only be able to devote one day here. With this in mind, suggestions for a one-day visit are included in Chapter 1.

concept of using Dresden as a focal point, this handbook provides guidance on sights both in Dresden and in the surrounding Saxony state of Germany.[3]

Area Covered in this Guide: While the focus, and majority of coverage in this guide is on the city of Dresden, several other enjoyable locales are presented as well. Each of these destinations may be reached easily from Dresden and, in many cases, by local train or tram services. In all cases, a trip to these attractive and varied destinations may easily be done in a relaxing day.

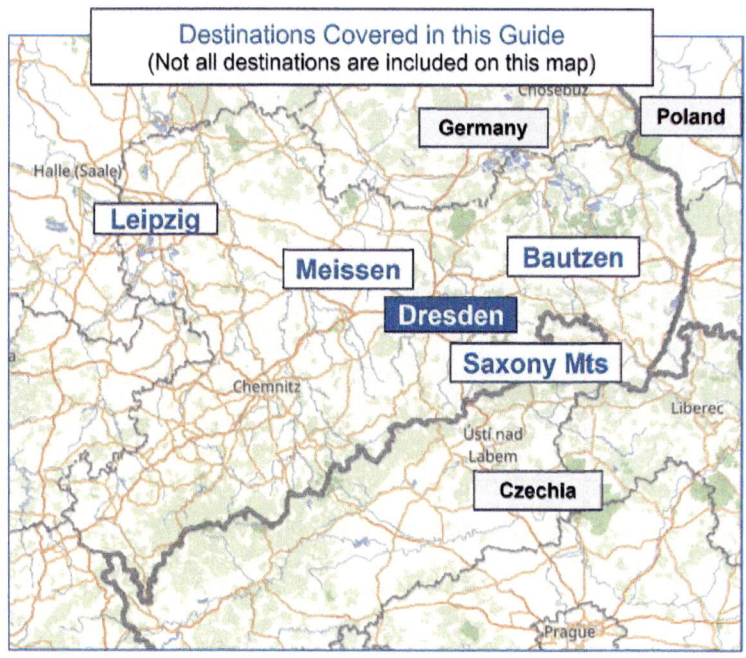

---

[3] **Dresden and Saxony:** Dresden is the capital of the German State of Saxony.

Destinations Covered in this Guide	
(In addition to Dresden)	
Locale	**Nature of Locale**
Bautzen	Attractive, walled town with numerous towers.
Leipzig	City – with good mix of old and new.
Meissen / Meißen	Attractive riverfront town with castle.
Moritzburg	Baroque Palace
Pillnitz	Palace – Near Dresden
Saxon Switzerland	Mountain area with beautiful rock formations and large castle.
Weesenstein	Castle

Itinerary Suggestions: If your travel schedule allows, plan on staying at least 2 nights in Dresden. Ideally, you will be able to stay as many as three nights.

This is an area with a wonderful variety of sights outside town such as the many castles or the rugged beauty of the Saxon Switzerland National Park. Two or more days are needed to gain even a moderate understanding of what this area has to offer.

Strive to leave one day open and unplanned near the end of your stay. Build in a day in which you have not pre-booked any excursions or planned major activities. The reason for this is that, once there, you will discover places which you either want to revisit or learn about new places which appeal to you. If you have a full schedule, you will lose this luxury.

One Day in Dresden & Saxony: If your schedule only allows for one day here, such as this being one stop for a river cruise, you will have many options for how to fill your day. Three alternatives are outlined below. Unfortunately, these options are generally mutually exclusive as a full day is required for each of them.

- Focus on Central Dresden – For most individuals, spending a day exploring the heart of Dresden will be a logical course of action. Depending on your preferences, there is no shortage of sights such as museums, cathedrals, intriguing streets, and shopping. Chapter 4 outlines the leading points of interest here. Exploring central Dresden can easily be done on foot for most of us and there are many walking tours available. A good add-on would be taking the Hop-On Bus tour which would give you a broader feel for this city.

- Head to the mountains of Saxon Switzerland – Roughly a forty-five-minute drive from central Dresden is the Bohemian and Saxon Switzerland National Park. It is a rugged set of hills with intriguing structures and natural formations such as the Bastei Bridge. More details on this are available in Chapter 10. Numerous tours from Dresden are available and most tours require a full day. A must-see for nature lovers. Expect to do some hiking on this day.

- Castles and Palaces: The Saxony state has numerous castles and palaces to explore. The various Dukes of Saxony built many palaces, mostly Baroque style, which are easy to reach and explore. Actually, one of the larger palaces is Dresden Castle, which is right in the heart of town. It allows you to combine this event with exploring other Old Town attractions. Other important palaces and castles such as the one in Meissen are a bit further afield and a short drive or tour will be required. Guidance on the most notable palaces in Saxony may be found in Chapter 10.

Consider a City, Area, or Museum Card: When staying in a city filled with attractions, purchasing a City Card can be advantageous.

In Dresden, there are different cards on offer ranging from a traditional City Card to a Regional Card (Regio Card) which includes area travel. Do

not acquire one if you only want to visit one or two attractions during your stay.

These passes can always be purchased in the Tourist Office and are available online prior to your trip. When visiting Dresden, you will have the option of purchasing the City Card or Regional Card in increments of 1, 2, or 3 days. See chapter 8 for details.

Visit the Tourist Office: Dresden' main Tourist Information Office is conveniently located. It is situated in the heart of Old Town

Dresden Tourist Office Website:
www.Dresden.de

The Tourist Center is in the heart of Old Town - facing the historic Neumarkt.
Photo source: Google Earth

Preface

(Altstadt) next to the Neumarkt Plaza. There is also an office in the main train station.

You can obtain information on available tours and places to visit. Even if you have done substantial research prior to your trip, it is likely you will learn of opportunities which you had not previously uncovered.

Download Some Apps: With the incredible array of apps for Apple and Android devices, almost every detail you will need to have a great trip is available up to and including where to find public toilets. The following are a few apps used and recommended by the author. [4]

- Dresden App: This is the official app for Dresden provided by the city and tourist office. It details attractions, museums restaurants, and transportation. Caution, some portions are only available in German.

- DVB Mobil: The official app for the area's transportation system. An excellent tool to see routes and schedules and real time availability. Also, use this to purchase tickets and passes.

- Dresden Transit Maps: Another detailed (although a bit complex) app to use for the area's transportation network.

The DVB App is a helpful tool to learn and use Dresden's transportation

---

[4] **General Travel Apps:** There are numerous excellent travel apps to select from. The ones cited here are recommended by the author, but your search for helpful apps should not be limited to this.

- Dresden Map and Walks: This firm creates apps for numerous cities which detail suggested walks to discover the city along with detailed maps.
- German for Beginners: A good way to pick up some basic terminology while in Dresden and Germany.
- Rome2Rio: An excellent way to research all travel options including rental cars, trains, flying, ferries, and taxis. The app provides the ability to purchase tickets directly online.
- Flush: Easily find public restrooms/toilets when that need arises.
- Trip Advisor: Probably the best overall app for finding details on most hotels, restaurants, excursions, and attractions.

1: Dresden – The Capital of Saxony

Dresden is a beautiful miracle of a small city. Yes, this city of over 700,000 in the metro area has the usual array of a charming old town, a scenic river, world-class museums, and intriguing streets to explore. But, when you consider that after WWII, much of Dresden was little more than rubble and that some of it was rebuilt inside of East Germany during the Stalin era, seeing this beauty takes on a whole new meaning.[5]

Dresden and the River Elbe

---

[5] **Rebuilding after German Unification:** Many of the more impressive sites such as Frauenkirche Baroque Church were not rebuilt until after German reunification in 1990.

Although Dresden has several impressive museums and historic sights, the real star of the show is the city center itself. If you do nothing more than just take time to admire the architectural beauty of central Dresden, you will come out a winner. When visiting here, strive to just amble slowly through Old Town (Altstadt), admire your surroundings, sit and have a coffee (or beer – this is Germany after all), and take some photos. Then, head off to view some sights which are of interest to you, many of which are outlined in chapters 4, 5, and 6 of this guide.

Dresden Rebuilt
Structures such as these on the Neumarkt Square may look old but they were rebuilt from scratch (rubble) after WWII.
Photo source: Jorg Blobelt - Wikipedia

What to Expect: If your focus is on the historic center then you will encounter a city which is easy to explore on foot as most of it is level. There is a large plaza, the Neumarkt, which is a perfect

---

[6] **Neumarkt and Old Town:** The term Neumarkt (New Market) can be a little confusing as it is actually in the heart of Altstadt (Old Town).

locale to start your explorations. Most of the leading attractions are in Old Town, or the left bank, Dresden. The specific neighborhood is called "Innere Altstadt." This is also where many hotels, restaurants, and leading shops may be found.

> Most of central Dresden is **pedestrian friendly** with minimal traffic around you.

This section of town measures only about 2/3 of a mile wide and 1/3 of a mile deep (as measured from the river). Put another way, unless you have mobility concerns, exploring this area is easy to do in a one-day visit and you may do so on foot. There are, of course, notable attractions outside of the Old Town and many of these are cited in Chapters 5 and 6.

Dresden and Brühl's Terrace
Along the river is an expasive barrier Brühl's Terrace with grand entry ways through it into Old Town.
Photo source: Max A - Wikipedia

If you are arriving by River Cruise, you are in luck as most boats dock just two or three blocks from the Neumarkt plaza.

There is a large, fortified wall, Brühl's Terrace[7], which separates the river from the city, providing for a dramatic entrance as you cross under it to enter Old Town.

Across the River Elbe is New Town (Neustadt) which is a pleasant neighborhood and easily reachable by a long bridge, but there is little here in the way of attractions. Note one big exception to this is the shoreline along the Right Bank where New Town is. It is your best opportunity for photos of historic Dresden and the many boats along the river.

Overview of Dresden & Saxony: Dresden has been nicknamed "Florence on the Elbe" due to the many beautiful and often Baroque-styled structures similar to that found in Florence, Italy. Many resources label Dresden as a "Baroque City." That moniker does not do justice to the city as there are prominent structures in other architectural styles including many in the Renaissance style and even several post-modern buildings.

In size, Dresden is Germany's 12th largest city with a city population of roughly 590,000.

The Royal Palace in Dresden
Photo source: Dennis Jarvis - Wikimedia

---

[7] **Brühl's Terrace:** Information on this prominent site, and other points of interest in Dresden may be found in Chapter 4.

Put another way, it doesn't show up on the top ten lists of German cities by size. This notably smaller size when compared to such cities as Berlin or Munich, provides for a more relaxed and intimate feel.

When considering tourism, Dresden takes on a slightly different perspective as it is a very popular destination. Depending on which source you review, Dresden ranks around the 5th or 6th most visited city in Germany.[8] This mid-range ranking for tourism is a good thing as there are many services here geared to servicing visitors, but not so many that you feel overwhelmed.

The River Elbe bisects Dresden
Old Town/Altstadt is on the Left Bank
New Town/Neustadt is on the Right Bank

Like many cities, Dresden is largely defined by its river and topography. The Elbe River, which is navigable by river boats and

---

[8] **Visitor Ranking Resource:** A great resource for reviewing the most popular destinations in Germany (and other areas) is www.WorldAtlas.com. An overview of each city is provided citing attractions to consider and what the draws of each city are.

barges, enables smaller commercial vessels to reach both the North Sea (a bit over 200 miles north) and Prague. The large Dresden Basin and Elbe Valley is a fertile, forested area and this led to much of the early settlement. It was also advantageous that the Elbe River was relatively easy to cross in the area of Dresden.

Dresden is the capital of the German state of Saxony. It was officially established as the capital by Napoleon in 1806. At that time, it was designated as the Kingdom of Saxony. Other notable cities are in this state with Leipzig being the biggest. Dresden is the second largest city in this state.[9]

---

[9] **Visiting Leipzig and other Saxony Cities:** Day trips via train to area cities including Leipzig are easy to do. Chapter 10 provides guidance for visiting these cities.

Layout of Dresden: Although Dresden is fairly spread out, most points of interest, shops, and lodging of interest to casual visitors will be found in two neighboring areas. These two sectors of town have been cited several times in this guide already as "Old Town" and "New Town." These aren't the only neighborhoods of course as the city has incorporated many neighboring communities.

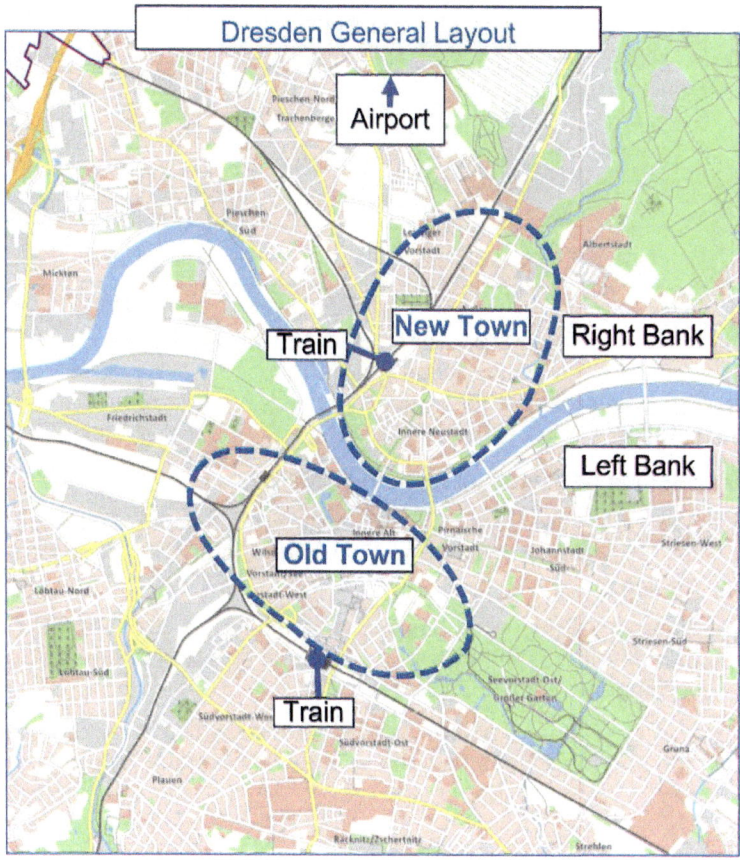

Old Town: In German "Altstadt." You may also see the name "Inner Altstadt" which can lead to some confusion. Each district has various subsets and the small "Inner/Innere" Altstadt is a part of

Central Dresden is a pleasant maze to explore.

the larger Old Town area. For most of us, this is where a majority of your time and explorations will be focused as it includes the leading points-of-interest, major shopping, and even the primary train station.

Some of the treasures found here include:[10]

- The Church of Our Lady – Dresden Frauenkirche – a beautiful, domed church which is a defining element of Dresden's skyline.

- Neumarkt Square – A bustling center in the heart of Old Town is lined with restaurants and museums. This is also where you will find the Tourist Office.

- Zwinger Palace – a large, ornate complex which includes several notable museums such as the Old Masters Picture Gallery.

---

[10] **Old Town Points of Interest**: These are all detailed further in Chapter 4 of this guide along with several others.

- Procession of Princes – A strikingly complex tile mural which is over 100 meters long. It details the history of the Saxony ruling family.

- Brühls Terrace & Dresden Fortress: Early city walls built to protect Dresden. This impressive structure not only provides excellent views of the river, but also includes the Dresden Fortress below the terrace.

- The Royal Palace – A 15th century palace which now houses several museums. This is a Baroque masterpiece which is open to tours.

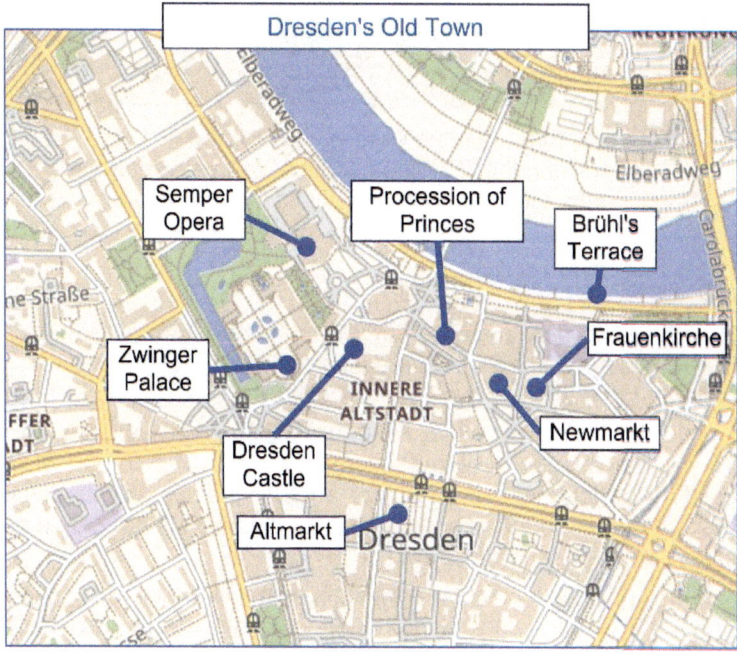

Several more notable points of interest may be found in Old Town, and they are outlined further in this guide. This area is also where the city's most notable train station is located along with some of the better shopping opportunities.

For some fun - head across the river to New Town where you will find the "Canaletto-Blick." A great way to get some interesting photos of Old Town Dresden.

New Town / Neustadt: The Right Bank area of central Dresden is known as Neustadt with the easiest-to-reach neighborhood carrying the name of Innere/Inner Neustadt.

This area of town, while historically older than Altstadt (Old Town), has a newer feel and layout as a result of a complete rebuild in the late 17th century after a major fire. So, in this case, "new" means that many of the buildings and streets are only a bit older than four hundred years.

The appeal here differs dramatically from Old Town. Where Old Town holds a majority of prominent and historically significant structures, New Town is more a day-to-day area with offices, apartment blocks, broad avenues, and parks. This does not mean that the area is boring, it isn't. If you enjoy active nightlife, this is the area to visit.

Dresden's New Town / Neustadt is characterized by broad avenues, apartment blocks, and small parks.

This area is often labeled as the "artisan" sector of town as many galleries and coffee shops may be found here. Consider this area to be a perfect escape from the tourist-centric Old Town and a great place to find almost every variety of dining.

Some of the leading points of interest in New Town include:

- Golden Horseman Statue: Often cited as the Golden Rider. A striking, life size statue in bright gold dedicated to King August II of Saxony.
- Neustadt Market Hall: A great place to go shopping for local goods in a covered shopping center. Ornate interior with wrought-iron stairs and railings.
- Pfunds Dairy: Interestingly this specialty dairy store has been labeled by Guiness Records as "The most beautiful dairy shop in the world." Incredibly ornate with stoneware floor and counter by Villeroy and Boch.
- Museum of Military History: A contemporary structure with over a million items on detailing Germany's military history.

Dresden and WWII: This city suffered one of the most profound and horrific events of the war. Curiously, Dresden largely escaped being attacked for most of the war. In February 1945, in the closing months of the war, the city was firebombed by the Allies and over ninety percent of the city center was destroyed and roughly 25,000 people killed.

There were four bombing raids in total over a two-day period in February with almost 3,000 tons of bombs dropped. Later, in early March of 1945, two more raids were conducted. These bombings were conducted for several reasons, chief among them was the existence of a substantial rail system here and over 100 German factories engaged in war time production. To many, the greatest puzzle about these bombings was why it took so long for them to occur, given that so many neighboring areas had been repeatedly bombed. The war came to an end less than three months later.

Dresden Frauenkirche Church
Before the Bombing - After the Bombing

Looking at "then and now" photos of the city, it is amazing to see what the city was like after the bombings in 1945 vs. the current existence of pristine and beautiful structures such as the Baroque Frauenkirche Church building. Even today, however, when you stroll the streets, you can still find black marks from the fires which occurred as a result of the bombings.

Dresden after the Fire Bombings
Dresden was in complete ruins after the 1945 bombings.
Photo source: Wikipedia

Some Interesting & Varied Facts About Dresden:

- Devastating Fires: WWII wasn't the only time this city was heavily damaged by fire. In 1491, the majority of the small city was destroyed by a fire. After that time, the city was modernized to the standards of that time and many of the new build-Fings were crafted in a Renaissance style.

- Communism and Saxony: After WWII, the area was part of Eastern Germany and under Communist rule and Stalin. Large sectors of the city were rebuilt during this time and done so with a mixture of unattractive Stalinist era apartment blocks along with a rebuild of several historically prominent structures such as the Zwinger palace.

- Relative Size: This is the 12th largest city in Germany and is not even the largest city in Saxony. Dresden's neighbor

Leipzig is Saxony's biggest city. This is also the second largest city on the river Elbe.

- A Green City: Dresden is one of Europe's greenest cities. Over sixty percent of the city area is covered with parks, large and small. There are even expansive wooded areas here and in the surrounding Elbe Valley which provide enjoyable hiking opportunities.

- Dresden, Saxony, and Royalty: This city and state has been the seat of various ruling families for centuries. The most notable rulers were the Kings of Saxony who ruled from 1806 until WWI. Be sure to visit the Fürstenzig – or "Procession of Princes" in Dresden. This is an incredible 102-meter-long porcelain mural depicting the history of the area's rulers.

- Dresden Porcelain: One product which is synonymous with the city of Dresden is fine porcelain. Today, porcelain made in the Dresden area but under the name of Meissen Porcelain, is still available. There is a factory to visit along with an extensive museum just a few miles outside of Dresden. Check www.Porzellan-Museum.com for details. There is also a store in central Dresden.

- Enjoy Sports?: Even if you are not a total sports fanatic, it can be fun to go to a soccer/football stadium to watch the local team play. In Dresden, the team is "Dynamo Dresden." Their stadium, Rudolf-Harbig Stadion, which holds over 30,000 fans, is just a short distance south from central Dresden. Take a look at www.Dynamo-Dresden.de for details.

- Economy and Leading Industries: Dresden was slow to recover economically, even after reunification. Today, this is an active center for electronics and pharmaceuticals. Some of the leading firms with large operations here include: Volkswagen, AMD – a leader in semiconductors, and Glaxo Smith Kline who has a large pharmaceutical works complex.

- Universities: Several universities are located here. The Dresden University of Technology is among the ten largest in

Germany with a student enrollment of over 30,000. There are five large universities here.

- Products Invented Here: We don't really think much about where most products we use were invented, but as you stroll the streets of Dresden, consider that products such as toothpaste and even coffee filters had their start here. Some sources also state that milk chocolate had its start here, but this is hard to verify.
- The World's Most Beautiful Milk Shop: Stroll on over to Old Town to visit the Pfunds Dairy shop. It is elaborate to say the least with walls covered in decorative tiles. See Chapter 5 for more details.

2: When to Visit
Climate & Major Events in Dresden and Saxony

Climate in Dresden and Saxony: A majority of the year here can have pleasant weather. Winter is naturally the least hospitable season but, even that is not horrible (it isn't fun either). In the summer, the conditions are most likely to be warm with some humidity. Broiling hot conditions are not the norm. Officially this is termed to be a "moderately Continental climate.

Dresden in the Spring
Springtime is a great time to visit the city and do so with minimal tourist crowding.

Winter: Expect cold and snowy conditions during much of December to mid-February. Often cold air will find its way here from as far as Siberia. The biggest positive here during winter is the lack of crowds. The negatives, in addition to the cold, are grey and cloudy conditions. If your focus is on visiting museums, then you won't have any problems, especially given the reduction in tourism.

Spring: Once the calendar reaches early April, the conditions for visiting will likely be pleasant although cool-to-cold and rain is likely. Put another way, be sure to have a mid-weight jacket with a hood with you. For the author, this is a near-perfect time to visit the area as many tours are starting up, the temps are tolerable, tourist crowds are moderate, and hotel prices are not yet at their summer highs.

Summer: Dresden is a popular destination which is good and bad. The negatives are increased crowds and prices. All tours will be up and running. The weather in the region can be warm and muggy but not horrible. Surprisingly, the nights can be a bit cool. Rain showers are frequent so having a light jacket is a reasonable precaution.

Fall: September to early October can bring near perfect conditions although rain showers are still common. Expect warm, but not hot weather. Crowding in September is still notable but, by October this, along with hotel prices, will be on the decline.

Saxony Average Area Climate by Month [11]			
Month	Avg High	Avg Low	Avg Precip
Jan	37 F / 3 C	28 F /-2 C	2.4 inches
Feb	40 F / 4 C	29 F /-2 C	2.2 inches
Mar	47 F / 9 C	34 F /1 C	2.1 inches

---

[11] **Weather Resource**: All climate data cited here is from Wikipedia.com

Saxony Average Area Climate by Month [11]

Month	Avg High	Avg Low	Avg Precip
Apr	58 F /14 C	41 F /5 C	1.8 inches
May	66 F /19 C	48 F /9 C	2.4 inches
Jun	72 F /22 C	54 F /12 C	2.6 inches
Jul	76 F /25 C	58 F /14 C	2.9 inches
Aug	76 F /24 C	57 F /14 C	3 inches
Sep	66 F /19 C	51 F /10 C	2.4 inches
Oct	56 F /14 C	44 F /7 C	2.5 inches
Nov	46 F /8 C	36 F / 2 C	2.5 inches
Dec	39 F / 4 C	31 F /-1 C	2.8 inches

The Saxon Switzerland National Park
Visit this natural delight near Dresden in the Fall to view a stunning landscape.

Major Festivals and Events in & near Dresden: There are several popular events in this area each year. Visiting one of these can be a great addition to your stay. The only downsides are the added crowds in Dresden and increased lodging rates. Information on some of the leading events follows. (This is not a complete list of all events.).[12]

When	Event
Mid-April	Filmfest Dresden
Mid-May	Dixieland Festival Dresden
May to June	Dresden Music Festival
Late Nov thru Dec	Christmas Market

Dresden's Striezelmarkt
The focal point of this Advent/Christmas event is in the Altmarkt in Old Town Dresden.

---

[12] **Events in and near Dresden:** The area's tourist website, www.Dresden.de provides updated details on most events.

Filmfest Dresden: This is an international film festival focusing on short films and animations. It has been ongoing since 1989. This runs for five days in mid-April, and you can expect as many as 70 or 80 films from almost two dozen countries. The films which are shown are typically selected from thousands of entries.

In recent years, the films have been shown in over a dozen locations in and near Dresden, so checking the website for the current program is helpful. (Author's comment – this event site is not user friendly, and it takes some digging to get useful info.)

- Website: **www.Filmfest-dresden.de**

Dixieland Festival: Okay, you did not misread the title, and this isn't the south of USA or Disneyland. There really is a Dixieland festival here each May, and it is very popular with over 300,000 people attending. 2024 will be the 52nd event and it lasts for a full week.

Actually, this is something of an overgrown party with events throughout the city, parades, and even riverboats complete with Dixieland bands. Oh, there is one negative (for some)… people are having a good time and it can be a bit raucus.

- Website: **www.DixielandFestival-Dresden.com**

Dresden Music Festival: Just a couple of weeks after the Dixieland Festival is another popular music event in Dresden. This one provides for a completely different experience as the focus is more on symphonic music. The official name is "Dresdner Musikfestspiele" and the variety of music includes classical and even some jazz. There is some overlap in timing with the Dixieland Festival as this runs for nearly a month. The sixty or more concerts take place in over twenty venues across town, so checking the official program on their website is advised.

- Website: **www.Musikfestspiele.com**

The Dresden Christmas Markets: Dresden has a notable and popular Christmas market (set of markets actually). Most Germany Advent or Christmas markets go by the name "Weihnachtsmarkt" and this also applies to Dresden, but you may come upon the name of "Striezelmarkt" which is the specific name for this large event. This is one of the oldest such advent markets in Europe and has been occurring since 1434.The 2024 event will be the 590th occurrence.

The center of activities, food and gift stands may be found at the Altmarkt next to Old Town. For children, there are several special attractions such as a carousel, Ferris wheel, and fairytale tower.

- Website: **www.StriezelMarkt.Dresden.de**
- 2024 Dates: End of November to Dec 24

3: Traveling to Dresden

Located in Eastern Germany, near the Polish and Czech Republic borders, Dresden is a convenient stop on the route between Berlin and Prague. It is easily reachable by flying, train, driving, and even riverboat. This is a common stop for Elbe River boat tours. [13]

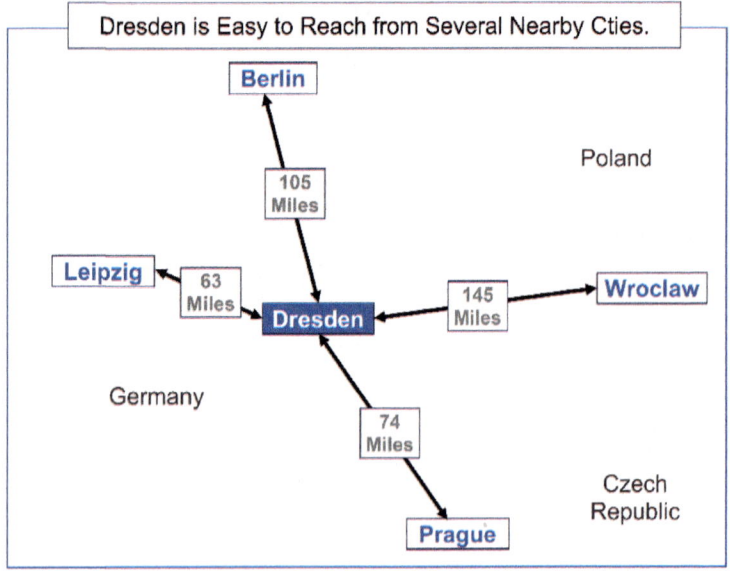

---

[13] **Distances Shown:** The distances shown on the above diagram are "as the crow flies" and will naturally vary based on your mode of transportation and your start and end points.

Travel Planning App: A great app or website to use is www.rome2Rio.com. One of the many plusses to this site is the ability to quickly compare options of traveling by: train, flying, bus, and driving. If you choose, you can also book travel directly from this site.

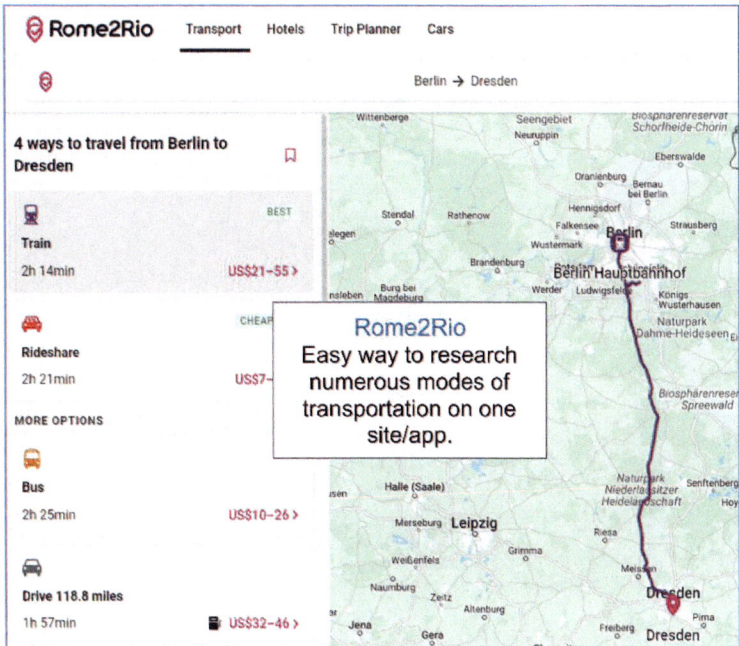

Rome2Rio
Easy way to research numerous modes of transportation on one site/app.

Arriving by Train: There are two train stations which service central Dresden.

Dresden Central Station / Dresden Hbf: In all probability, if you come to Dresden by train, this is the station you will arrive at. The station sits a bit less than a mile south of the heart of Dresden's Old Town and the

Direct Trains from Berlin

One caution – many (not all) routes to Dresden from central Berlin will require a change of trains along the way.

Neumarkt. This distance can be walked and, if you do so, this route will take you through the city's primary shopping district.

If you do not want to walk into the heart of town from the station, both the local bus and tram services stop here. (See Chapter 7 for guidance on the local transportation network).

Several shops and small restaurants are in the train station. Also, for possible lodging convenience, several hotels are in the immediate vicinity of this station. (Chapter 9 provides a list of suggested lodging).

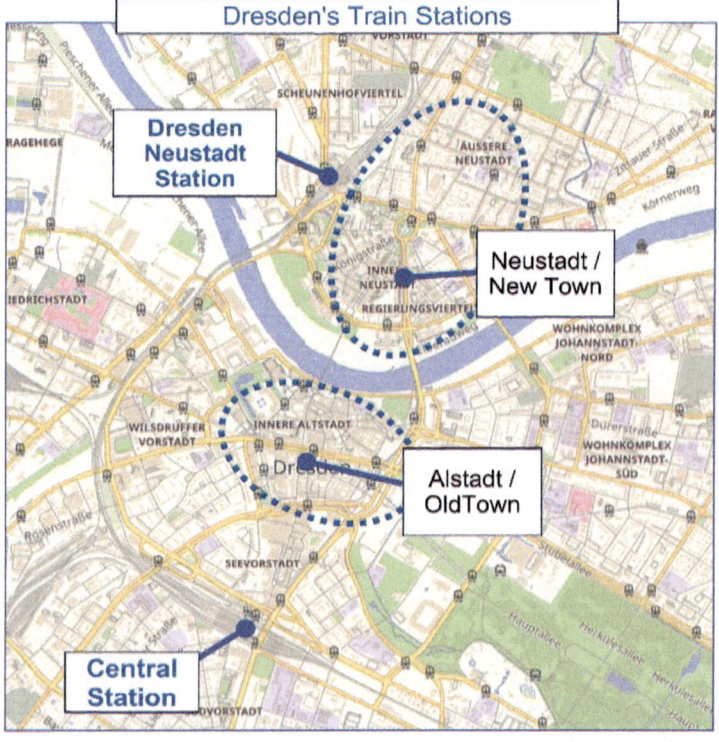

Dresden Neustadt Station / Bahnhof Dresden-Neustadt:
This secondary station is a good choice if your destination and/or lodging is in the New Town sector of Dresden. Otherwise, the Central Station tends to be the better option due to its proximity

to shopping and the heart of Old Town. The Dresden-Neustadt station is serviced by the local bus and tram system, so it is easy to catch a ride into most any area of town. Also, if you wish to walk into central Neustadt, it is only about a ten-minute walk to such locales as the Market Hall or even less to the Albertplatz. A good array of small shops and services are available in this station.

Booking Train Tickets. Given the popularity of travel to Dresden from Berlin and Prague, advance purchase should be considered, especially in high season. If you have not purchased train tickets in advance, convenient ticket booths are available at the train station.

Several online services are available to book in advance including:

- Bahn.de – Germany's national rail service and by far the most prominent. Using them provides the advantage of being able to make changes in the station if problems arise.

- Ticket Resellers – several online agencies allow you to book tickets through them and may provide the convenience of booking other forms of transportation or lodging at the same time. Leading resources for this include (And not limited to):
    - www.rome2Rio.com (Author favorite)
    - www.TrainLine.com
    - www.RailEurope.com

~ ~ ~ ~ ~ ~

Arriving by Air: The Dresden Airport, "Flughafen Dresden" is located just six miles north of the city. It is a modest-sized operation, so you won't be subjected to massive crowding if you fly in here.

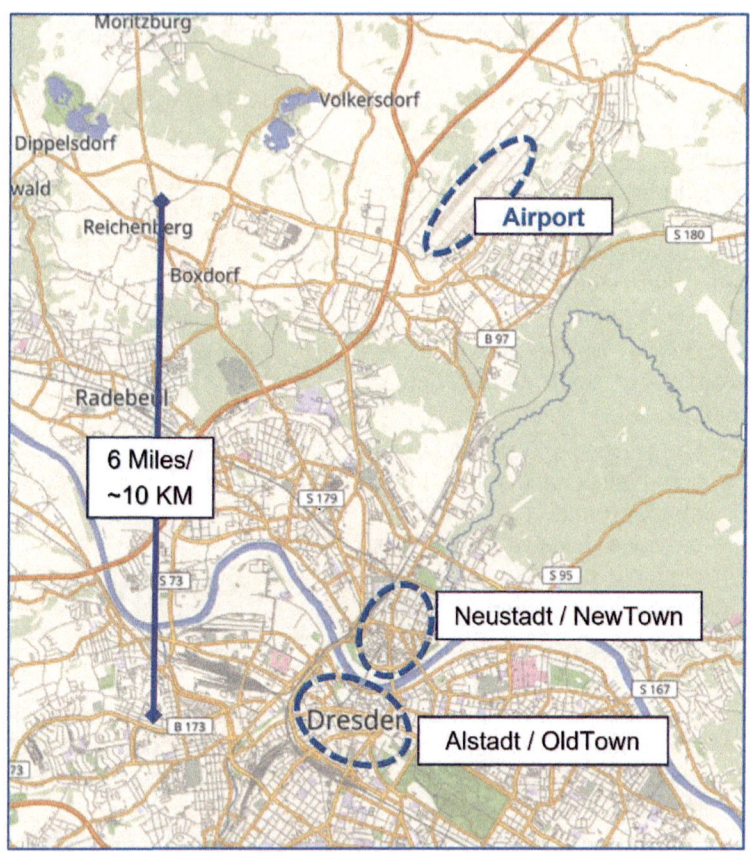

There are several options for simple travel into town from the airport but, note that the tram system does not service the airport.
- Train into town: The S-Bahn (In Germany, S-Bahn trains are suburban or regional in nature). Just below the main terminal is a train station where you can catch the S2 line into town. This route stops at both of Dresden's major train stations. Head to the "Dresden-Haupbahnhof" station if your

destination is Dresden's Old Town and historic center. This train departs about every thirty minutes and is a short ride. Tickets may be purchased at the station platform and no advance reservations are needed.

- Bus / Tram Combo: Buses depart right outside of the terminal. Look for either bus # 77 or 80. Both of these routes take you to nearby tram stops. From there, you may want to use the local tram app to determine which route to take. Or simply study the map which is posted at the tram station.
- Taxi: Several taxi companies service this airport, and during business hours, you can expect to find an available ride. Travel time, depending on your destination in town, will take around twenty minutes. If you wish to reserve a car or taxi in advance, consider one of the following:
  - Taxi Dresden – www.Taxi-Dresden.de
  - 8 X 8 Dresdner Chauffeur Service - www.8mal8.de
  - Taxi Schön - www.Taxi-Shuttle-ReiseService.de

Arriving by River Cruise: You are in luck. Almost every river cruise will dock right at the entrance to Old Town Dresden at Brühl's Terrace. You are, for all practical purposes, within a short walk to the majority of Dresden's treasures. For most individuals, there will be little need for additional transportation. So, enjoy.

4: Old Town Points of Interest

Museums, Cathedrals and Plazas in Central Dresden

The sights in Dresden range from the traditional and expected museums to unique treasures. We all have different preferences with some people preferring to spend their time in world-class museums while others are happy to just stroll the town to get a feel for it and perhaps do some people watching in the process. Listed here are a variety of attractions and there should be something here for everyone.

> **Dresden's Main Attraction is... Dresden**
> As with many cities in Europe, the main attraction is the town itself. Yes, there are some marvelous sights but don't forget to check out this town first by simply strolling around and exploring its avenues.

The number of sights in Dresden is surprisingly high with over twenty of them identified here. To help you locate a place of interest, these are organized into three geographical areas with a separate chapter for each area:

- Chapter 4 - Old Town / Altstadt: This is where a majority of the most notable attractions are. The area stretches from the river and includes the shopping areas near the train station.

- Chapter 5 - New Town / Neustadt: Dresden's right bank. Several attractions are here and are spread out some, generating a need to use public transport for many of the destinations.

- **Chapter 6 - Edge of Town**: Several attractions are close to both Altstadt and Neustadt but slightly further out. These are grouped here. Look for several prominent palaces here.

Dresden Points of Interest List		
Map #	Name	Type
Old Town / Altstadt Area		
1	Neumarkt	Town Square
2	Frauenkirche Dresden	Lutheran Church
3	Brühl's Terrace	City Wall & Promenade
4	Festung Dresden	Fortress & Multi-Media Tour
5	Procession of Princes	Large Outdoor Mural
6	Dresden Cathedral	Catholic Churuch
7	Zwinger	Palace & Museums
8	Dresden Castle	Residential Palace
9	Altmarkt-Galerie Dresden	Shopping Mall
10	Altmarkt	Plaza
11	Holy Cross	Church
12	Prager Straße/Strasse	Shopping Area
New Town / Neustadt Area – Chapter 5		
13	Golden Rider	Statue
14	Japanese Palace	Museum-Natural History
15	Neustadt Markthalle	Market Hall
16	Pfunds	Ornate Dairy Shop

Dresden Points of Interest List

Map #	Name	Type
Attractions A Bit Further Out from New and Old Town- Chp 6		
17	Military History Museum	German Military History
18	Schloss Albrechtsberg	Palace
19	Loschwitz	Funiculars
20	Hygiene Museum	German Hygiene Museum
21	Grosser Garten	Large Park with palace
22	Dresden Zoo	Zoo
23	Panometer	Multi-Media Experience

Old Town / Altstadt:

Consider starting your explorations at the prominent Neumarkt plaza and then venturing out from there. This is labeled number 1 on this list and all other district attractions are within an easy walk from here. The greatest distance is down to the shopping area and center near the train station.

This entire area measures roughly ½ mile square (a bit further if you head south to do some shopping or go to the train station). This is an easy area to explore on foot unless you have mobility limitations. It is flat but the pavers which are found in many areas can be a bit rough for some.

Another huge plus here is the limited automobile traffic, especially around the core of Old Town around the Neumarkt plaza. Also, this is one of the best areas to consider for lodging and many hotels are cited in Chapter 9 of this guide.

Old Town Dresden Points of Interest

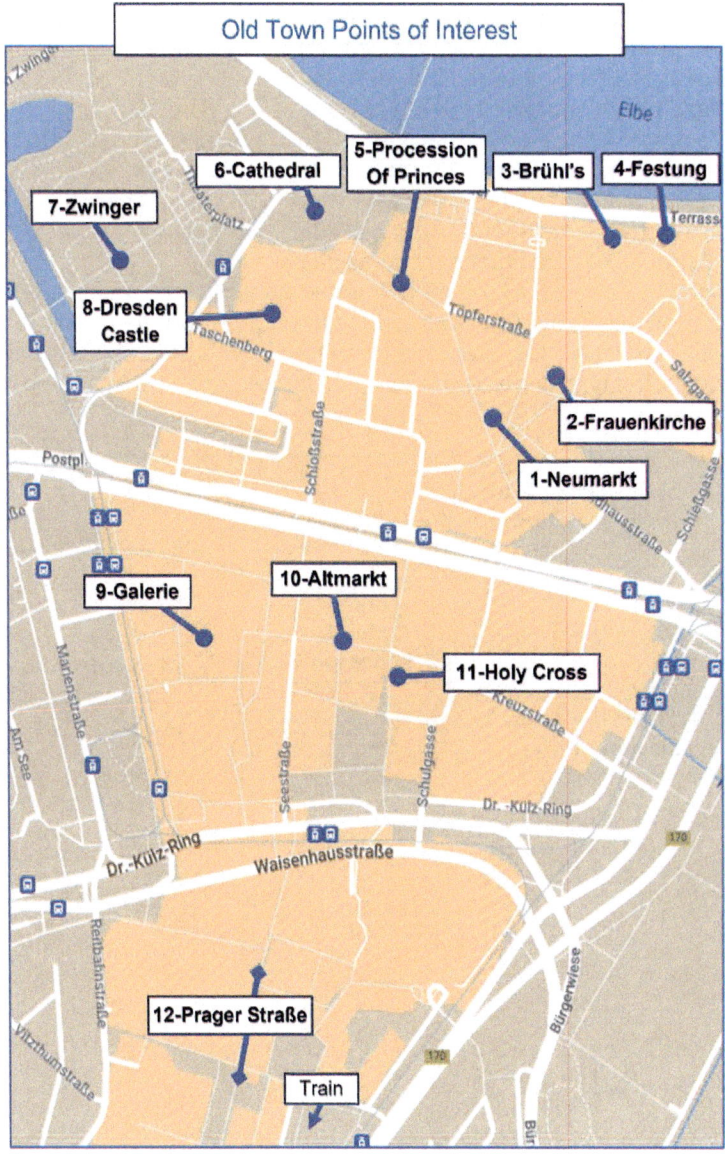

1 - Neumarkt Plaza: This is one of two prominent squares in the heart of Dresden. The other is the Altmarkt plaza which sits slightly south of here. Neumarkt Plaza dates back to 1548 and was noted for its Baroque-style buildings. Unfortunately, almost every building was destroyed during WWII. This absolute destruction makes the sights before you all the more impressive when you realize that it was all rebuilt over the decades following the war. The most notable structure, the Frauenkirche church, wasn't reopened until 2005. Today, this plaza is frequently the site of festivals and open markets.

> If you visit only one small part of Dresden, this square and the adjacent attractions should be it.

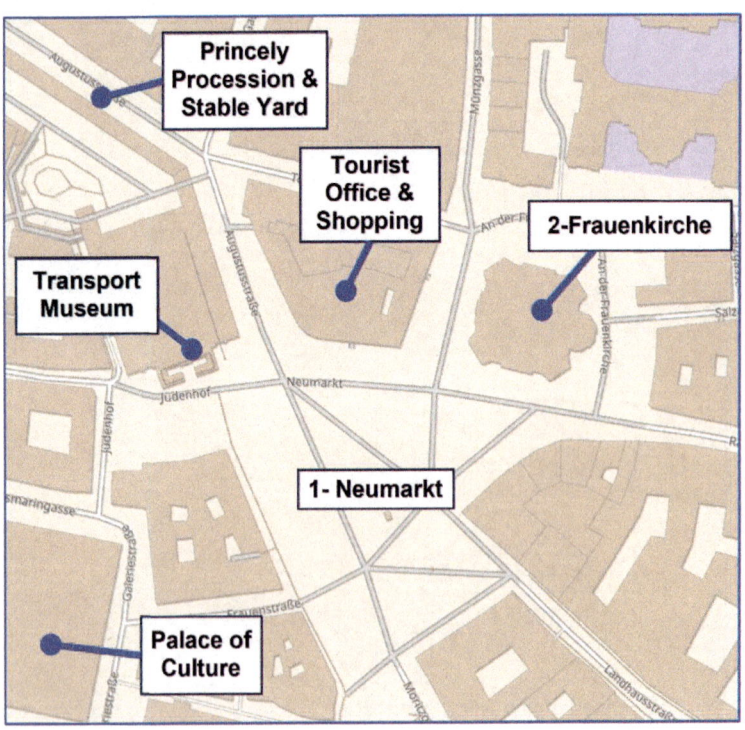

Old Town Dresden Points of Interest

Transportation to Here: This is largely a pedestrian-only sector of town so you will not find local transportation immediately at the plaza. However, just one block south both buses and trams stop here at the appropriately named "Altmarkt" stop.

What is Here: Several noteworthy structures line this plaza including:

- Martin Luther Statue: In the heart of the plaza is a monument to the religious and societal reformer Martin Luther. He lived and stayed here for roughly a year from 1516 to 1517. One fascinating aspect of this statue is it remained intact after the multiple bombings, even when everything around it was in ruins.

- Frauenkirche Dresden: This Baroque-styled Lutheran Church was left in ruins long after the WWII bombing raids. See further details on this iconic structure in the following pages of this chapter.

- Dresden Transport Museum / Verkersmuseum: Along the northwest section of this plaza is a large museum dedicated to all forms of transportation. Find full size train cars, vehicles, and even aircraft here. If you have a Dresden City Card, admission is included. (See Chapter 8 for details on this card). For full details on this museum go to: www:VerkersMuseum-Dresden.de.

- Tourist Office: Tucked back into the "Passage Dresden" shopping mall, is Dresden's Tourist Office. This is a good place to buy the City Card and gain insights into available tours.

- Stores and Restaurants: You don't have to go far to find shopping and dining once you are at Neumarkt. Along all sides of this plaza, you will find an expansive array of shops and restaurants.

The Neumarkt Plaza & Frauenkirche

2 - Frauenkirche Dresden: This Lutheran church, which is located on Neumarkt Square, is Dresden's most iconic structure. The current Baroque structure was first built in the early 18th century to replace a prior church. It has one of the largest domed ceilings in Europe. To many, given the struggles of the time between Protestants and Lutherans, this structure is a symbol of peace between the two groups.

The building which is here now is a nearly exact replica of the structure which had been destroyed during WWII. After the war, it was largely left in ruins and kept as a war memorial. It wasn't until the reunification of Germany that rebuilding was started. In 2005 the reconstruction was completed, and it was finally open to the public.

This is one of the highest and most visible structures in Dresden. The church, including the cross at the top, is 91 meters high (almost 300 feet). The dome tower also includes a set of bells and each has its own name and sound.

Tours and Visiting the Interior: Today, visitors are provided with several opportunities to explore and learn more about this church. Guided Tours are available as well as a museum in the lower level. Several tours are available including one which is a combination guided tour and prayer service.

Climbing to the Dome: One guided tour which is very popular is the ascent to the dome. These tours have a maximum of twenty-five people and can fill up quickly. Caution: there is a steep climb up 67 meters (about 220 feet), so some stamina and strong knees are needed.

Website: www.Frauenkirche-Dresden.de

Frauenkirche Church Interior

A Starting-Point Guide

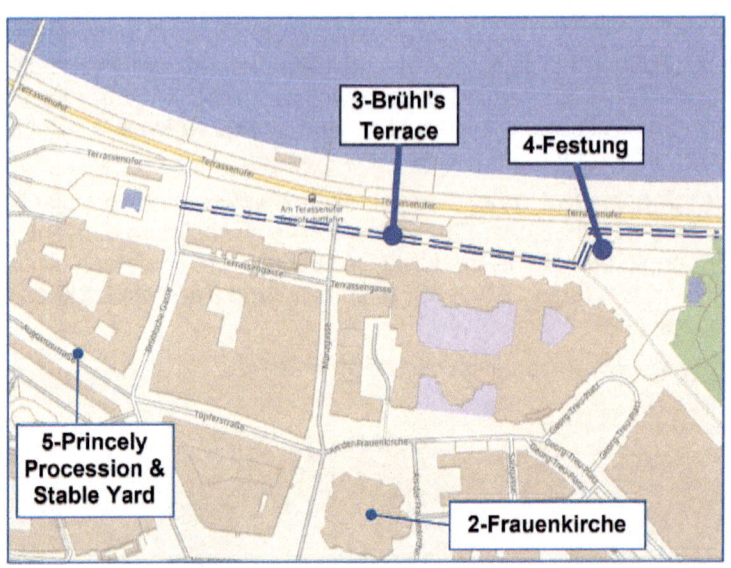

3 - Brühl's Terrace: This promenade (Brühlsche Terrasse in German) is one of Dresden's most popular spots, both for visitors and locals. Along what had once been the ramparts of the ancient city, this is a wide walkway which overlooks the Elbe River below. If you come here via a river cruise, chances are your boat will dock in the shadow of this impressive wall.

| Brühl's Terrace has the nickname of: "The Balcony of Europe" | This was first built in 1747 on top of the ancient city fortifications which dated back to the 16th century. Unfortunately, like so many other structures here, this was completely destroyed during WWII. It was rebuilt after the war to be a close (but not exact) match to what it was before the destruction. |

Along this walkway are several restaurants and outdoor cafés. If the weather is favorable during your visit, consider making this your lunch destination as the views across the river and of the river traffic are enjoyable. In addition to the eateries there are several notable features to watch for:

- Planetary Monument – The "Planetendenkmal" is midway along the terrace and is an interesting monument which depicts our planetary system.
- Public Restrooms – near the western end and down one level.
- Academy of Fine Arts – The Kunstakademie – this is one of several imposing structures devoted to the arts along this walk.
- Albertinum – the city's modern art museum. The building is done in a Renaissance Revival style.
- The Saxony Supreme Court – the Sekundogenitur.
- Brühlschen Garten – an enjoyable park with formal gardens and small ponds. This is a great spot to relax on a hot summer day.
- Dresden Fortress – Below the terrace are the remains of the ancient fortress and the "Dresden Xperience" which provides a unique multi-media experience. There is an elevator (near the park) which takes visitors down to this attraction.

Brühl's Terrace / The "Balcony of Europe"
Photo source: Nikater-Wikipedia

4 - Festung Dresden[14] / "Dresden Xperience": In the 16th century, the city of Dresden was a walled city with fortifications surrounding much of what is now known as the inner city. Today, most of those ancient walls and their gates are gone but, segments do remain and are largely under Brühls Terrace.

Dresden Xperience inside the Dresden Fortress
Photo Source: Festung Xperience

The best way to visit this historic facility is to visit the "Dresden Xperience." This attraction takes visitors through several sections of the fortress and provides a full 360 multi-media experience along the way. In the author's opinion, this really is a fun way to learn over traditional museums and provides for a lively experience.

The firm which developed this high-tech attraction has done so in several other locations including the Zwinger Palace and in

---

[14] **Dresden Fortress Museum:** Up until 2017, there was a traditional museum inside the ancient fortress below Brühl's Terrace. Recently this was converted to the new "Festung Xperience" described here. Several resources unfortunately still make reference to the former museum which can lead to some confusion.

Leipzig. There are no set showings so you may enter at any time and proceed on your own.

Duration: Allow for roughly an hour to visit and tour.

Hours: Closed Wednesday. Open most other days from 10AM to 6PM, but last admission time is 5 PM

Language: You will need to wear a headset when doing this tour. Several languages are available including English.

Cost: There is a €12 fee[15] for adults and €4.50 for children. If you have the local discount card, the Schloesserland Card, there is no entry fee. Consider purchasing tickets from the website in advance as this attraction can sell out during the summer season.

Website: www.Festung-Xperience.com

5 – Procession of Princes & Stable Yard / Fürstenzug & Stallhof:

- The "Procession of Princes" is an awe-inspiring tableau presenting the rulers of Saxony. Stretching 335 in width (102 meters) there are 23,000 porcelain tiles in this work of art.

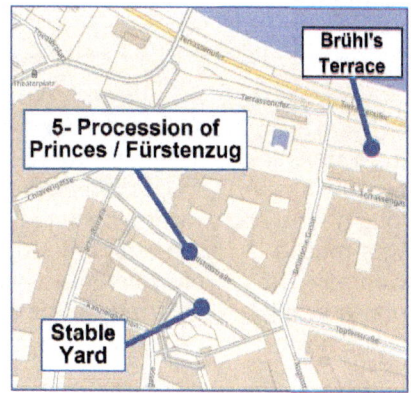

This is considered to be the largest porcelain artwork in the world. It displays the portraits of over 30 former dukes, kings, and other leaders of

---

[15] **Fee Note:** All fees cited in this guide are as of mid-2024 and are subject to change. Use the fees cited here as a general guideline only.

Saxony who were here between the early 12th century up to the start of the twentieth century.'

The "Procession of Princes" / Fürstenzug

There is no fee to view this impressive work of art and it is hard to miss as it sits between Brühl's Terrace and Neumarkt Plaza, two of Dresden's most prominent points. This work of art has a long history and was first done in the 16th century. In the 1870's it was redone in fresco and, unfortunately, this did not survive the weather. The current version was put in between 1904 and 1907 and amazingly it incurred only minor damage during the WWII firebombing.

Just over the wall from this artwork is another historic and somewhat artistic area, a former stable ground. The "Stallhof Dresden" is easy to miss as the primary entryway is through an archway near the southern end of the Procession of Princes. This building is part of the former residential palace and served as the site for royal equestrian tournaments and shows during the 16th century.

There is no fee to visit and, once you enter the courtyard, there are no shops or restaurants, so this will typically be a quick visit. However, the artistry of the main building is worth taking some time to enter and take some notable photos.

The Stable Yard / Stallhof

6 – Dresden Cathedral / Sanctissimae Trinitatis:[16] This Catholic cathedral dates back to 1739 and is a prominent feature along Dresden's waterfront skyline. This structure was built at a time when the city was primarily Catholic and at roughly the same time as the Frauenkirche Church which is on the Neumarkt plaza.

This was built in the Baroque style and is the largest church in Saxony and is over 270 feet tall. Along the outer balustrades,

---

[16] **Cathedral Names:** This cathedral, like many others, goes by several names so you may also find it referred to as The Cathedral of the Holy Trinity in Dresden or The Catholic Church of the Royal Court of Saxony.

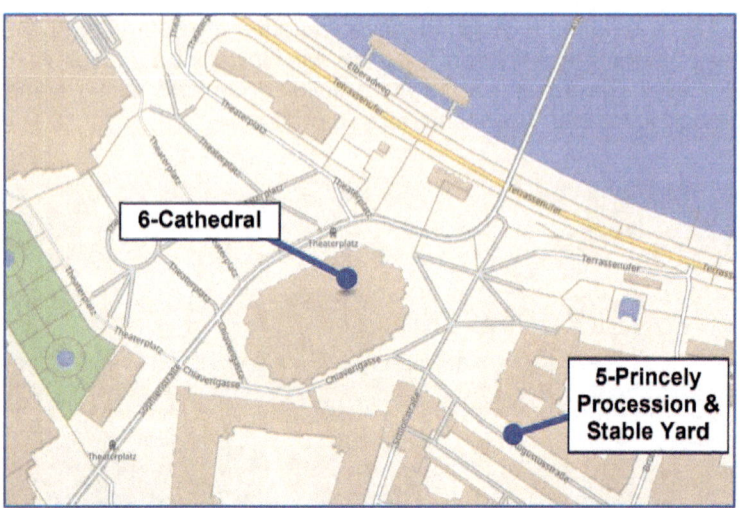

there are 78 statues, each nearly 10 feet tall. They represent a mixture of the Apostles, several saints, and even church dignitaries of the time.

When you examine the ornate exterior and interior, it is hard to imagine that this building suffered extreme damage during WWII and had to be rebuilt after the war. When it was rebuilt, this was done to match the structure before its near complete destruction.

Today, the church is open to visitors and the hours generally do not overlap when services are occurring.

Location: Schloßstraße 24, Dresden – fronting the river and the popular Schlossplatz plaza. Also, Brühl's Terrace has its start here.

Hours: Vary based on services. Most days it is open from 10AM to 5PM. Exceptions are Friday and Sunday, when it is not open until early afternoon.

Cost: There is no fee to enter the cathedral.

Website: www.Bistum-Dresden-Meissen.de

~ ~ ~ ~ ~

7 – Zwinger Palace / Dresdner Zwinger: This is a huge complex with a lot to see. You could easily spend a large part of a day exploring its museums and grounds.

Zwinger Palace / Dresdner Zwinger

A Starting-Point Guide

This is much more than just an impressive palace, make that a popular palace, as it is at or near the top of lists of most visited attractions here. When coming to the palace, you will soon find that this huge set of buildings also houses many of the region's most notable museums.

> **Fun Fact**
> The word "Zwinger" today in German literally translates to "Kennel." Clearly, this is one impressive kennel.

The palace itself was built in the early 18th century. It got its name not from a particular individual but, rather from how it is positioned between the fortress walls. During the Middle Ages, the term Zwinger was often used to define this secure section of a fortress between the inner and outer walls.

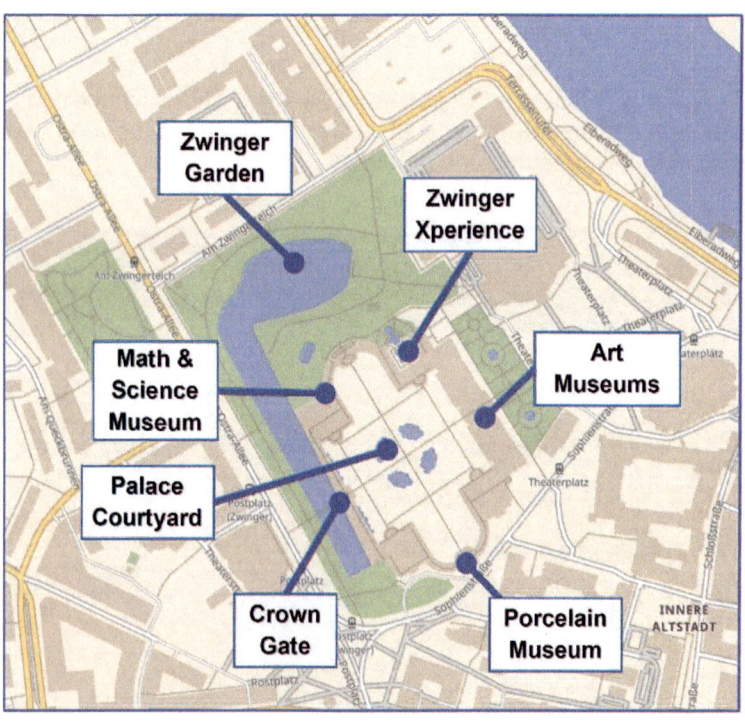

Palace History: This never fully functioned as a residential palace as was first intended. It was built during Germany's Baroque period and initially as an orangery, gardens, and festival area. There was to be a palace for Augustus the Strong in 1709 but that plan was abandoned after his death. This later evolved into a museum complex and has been the home of museums since it was rebuilt after WWII.

What is Here: The Zwinger complex is a set of six buildings / pavilions which are connected by various galleries. The interior grounds have large formal gardens and, from here, entrances to several museums. There is no charge to enter the grounds and explore and, for many, this will be enough. There are, however, several noteworthy museums inside of the pavilions.

- Crown Gate / Kronentor: An 18th century Baroque gateway topped with a large crown. It was built to be the primary and impressive entrance to the palace grounds.

Zwinger Crown Gate
Photo Source: Bybbisch94-Wikimedia Commons

- Gallery of Old Masters / Geräldegalerie Alte Meister: This art museum focuses solely on artists deemed "Old Masters", primarily from Dutch and Flemish schools. You may view over 700 works from such notables as Vermeer, Titian, and Tintoretto. There is a fee to enter the gallery. That one fee covers all of the museums within the Zwinger complex. Full details are available at: www.Gemaeldegalerie.skd.museum

- Sculpture Collection / SkulpturenSammlung: Adjoining the Old Masters Gallery is a museum focused on sculpture. There are two separate areas to view the collections with just the oldest sculptures held at Zwinger. Works from 1800 and later are on display in a museum with the name "Albertinum" and that facility is next to the small park adjacent to Brühl's Terrace. Inside the Zwinger galleries, are the sculptures which were crafted before 1800. Many of these date to antiquity including ancient Greece and Rome.

- Zwinger Xperience: A multi-media experience set inside the palace. It takes visitors through the history of Zwinger and what life was like when the palace grounds were used for festivals and parades. This interactive 360 display is one of two in Dresden with the other, the "Dresden Xperience," located under Brühl's Terrace. There is a fee to visit and the program takes about 45 minutes. Full details and ticket purchases may be done via the website: www.Zwinger-Xperience.com.

- Porcelain Collection / Porzellansammlung: In the early 1700's well-crafted porcelain, primarily from Asia, was very much in vogue. August the Strong, the king for whom the Zwinger Palace was created, not only started a porcelain factory in the area but, he also collected thousands of exquisite pieces, mostly from Japan and China. Today, over 20,000 pieces are held here. The museum is in the southeastern corner of the Zwinger complex and there is a modest fee to visit. It is closed on Monday.

> Museum Website
> The site:
> **www.Skd.Museum**
> provides a gateway to details on the Porcelain Museum, the Math Salon and several other local museums as well.

- Mathmatical Salon / Mathematisch-Physikalisher Salon: Despite the unusual title of "salon," this is a museum. The focus is on historic scientific instruments, telescopes, and even clocks. Roughly 500 instruments are on display. The museum is in the northeast pavilion and reachable from the courtyard. There is a small fee to enter. Like most museums in the area, it is closed on Monday.

~ ~ ~ ~ ~

Old Town Dresden Points of Interest

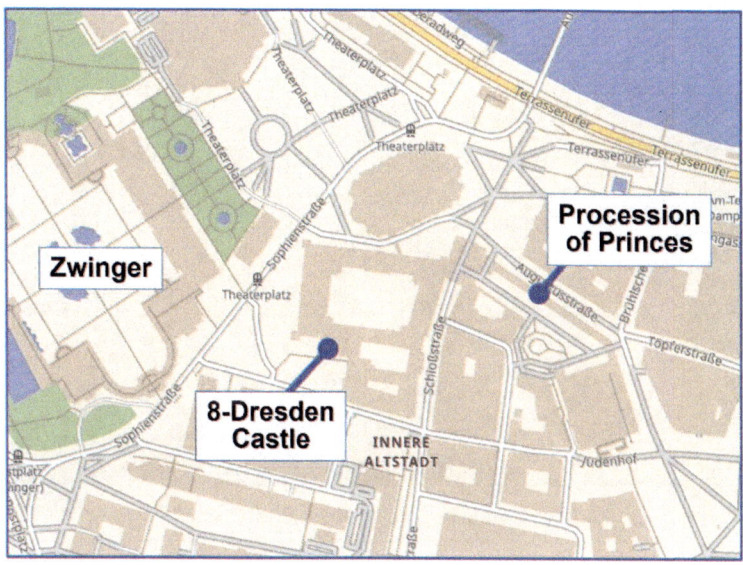

8 – Dresden Castle / Dresdner Schloss:[17] As you explore

Dresden's Old Town / Altstadt, it is easy to be amazed at the number of significant and historic structures which are packed into one small area. Sitting across the lane from the huge Zwinger Palace complex is yet another treasure, Dresden Castle. This was the home of both kings and electors (Electors can roughly be compared with Princes although they tended to have more power.)

This was a royal residence for nearly 400 years with the last

> **Palace Visitor Center**
> Understanding everything that is available here and the ticket options can be confusing. Consider stopping in at the palace visitor center at ground level of this massive complex to obtain tickets, book tours, and understand what the many museums have to offer.

---

[17] **Dresden Castle Name:** This magnificent structure is often cited as Dresden's "Royal Palace."

Dresdner Castle / Dresdner Residenzschloss

one there until 1918. Given that this huge structure of 500+ rooms evolved over the centuries (various leaders put their personal stamp on it over time), the architectural style is something of a mix with Baroque and Neo-Renaissance the most prominent. Also, this ornate structure was another casualty of WWII and much of it had to be rebuilt. The rebuilding largely did not happen until after German reunification. Even today, work is ongoing, and it was as recently as 2019 that another section, the State Apartments, was open to the public.

Today, much of the castle is open to the public and tours are available. There are also several museums to view here including:

- The Green Vault: A museum displaying much of the treasury of August the Strong. As early as the 1700's, this vault was kept as a clean area in which visitors were limited in quantity

> Museum Website
> The site is the same one used for the Zwinger Museums.
> **www.Skd.Museum**
> This website provides a good level of details for all museums both in the Castle and in the Zwinger complex. One caution – there is a lot here and some digging may be needed.

and cleanliness was required even back then. Today, visitors may view five rooms, each with different themes. There is a fee to enter and that fee also includes other museums here. Tours are presented via audio headsets. Closed on Tuesday.

- Royal State Apartments: This is a set of rooms inside the Royal Palace which were the living quarters for August the Strong, one of the region's most noted Kings. These were just reopened in 2019 after near complete destruction in WWII. Today, visitors are able to view how these royals lived. In addition to living quarters, the royal audience chamber and banquet halls are open to view. The tour also includes displays of ornate porcelain created in the porcelain factory which the king had initiated. Tours are available and the ticket cost of 14 Euro (as of Jan 2024) covers all museums within the Royal Palace.

- Rifle Gallery & Armoury: A gallery and museum focused on the evolution of weapons dating from medieval times. Exhibits are found on two floors with the most notable in the room called the "Long Hall."

The Armory / Rifle Gallery within Dresden Castle
Photo Source: SchiDD - Wikipedia

9 – Altmarkt-Galerie Dresden: Located a short stroll south from the Neumarkt plaza (a suggested starting point for your Dresden explorations) is one of two recommended shopping areas in this guide. Given the close proximity to the heart of Dresden's historic center, there is a surprising change in character as this area feels like a modern city center.

The Altmarkt-Galerie Dresden is an excellent shopping destination IF you are looking for "normal" shopping such as department stores, jewelry, clothing stores, and more. There are roughly two hundred stores here on two levels spread over a multi-block complex. This is generally not a good destination for souvenirs.

There is also an unending array of restaurants here from fast food to upscale. Look for dining not only in the shopping mall but in the busy Postplatz avenue which sits on the west side of the mall. The Altmarkt plaza sits alongside this shopping mall, so it is very easy to combine a visit both of them.

Getting Here: A short 6- or 7-minute walk south from Neumarkt and only slightly longer to Zwinger. If you wish to take the tram, several lines stop here – and either the Altmarkt or Postplatz stops work equally well.

> **Altmarkt Hotel Recommendation**
> Given the nearly unending array of shops, bars, and restaurants here along with proximity to a majority of the city's historic treasures, consider booking lodging at one of the many hotels in the Altmarkt Plaza area. Chapter 9 of this guide provides further insights.

When Open: Please note that this mall, along with many other shops in Dresden, is closed on Sunday.

Mall Website: www.Altmarkt-Galerie-Dresden.de

Old Town Dresden Points of Interest

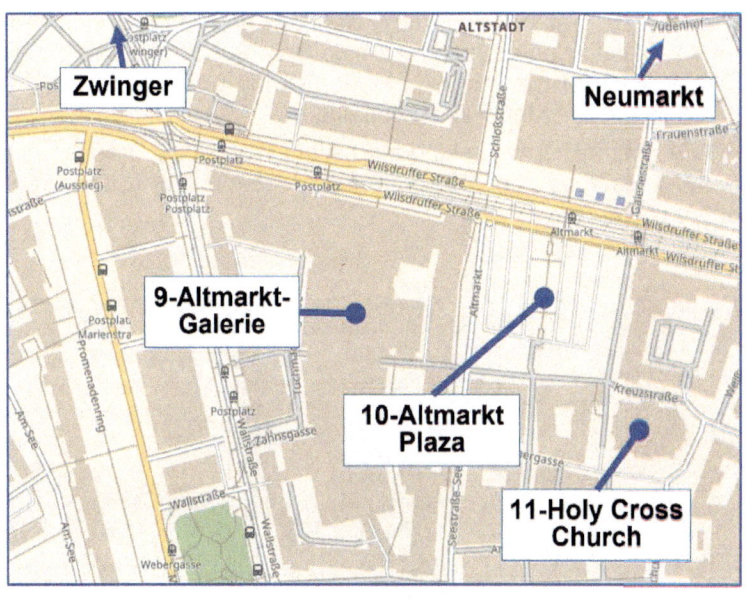

10 – Altmarkt: This plaza probably shouldn't be listed among the attractions within central Dresden due to the limited nature of what is here. It is included because of the many popular festivals held here and the central locale. If you arrive here during a time when no festivals or open markets are in progress, there really is not a lot to see and do here.

This plaza, which is a bit over 3 acres in size, dates back to the 14th century and was used for events and even circus grounds. It was largely replaced in importance when the Neumarkt square was opened in the middle of the 16th century.

> Driving to here?
>
> If you have a car while here, there is a large car park underneath the Altmarkt Plaza. This locale makes for a central spot to leave your vehicle while visiting the city.

Today, the plaza is lined with restaurants and hotels (See Chapter 9). Many open markets are held here on an ongoing basis. One building of note, which sits across the busy road from the plaza, is the Dresden Palace of Culture.

This plaza and the neighboring Altmarkt-Galerie Dresden are easy to reach by tram. The Altmarkt tram stop is directly in front of the plaza.

Altmarkt Plaza
The site of many festivals such as Dresden's Christmas Market

11 – Holy Cross Church / Kreuzkirche Dresden: Located close to the Altmarkt Plaza is an impressive, spired, Lutheran Church. This is the largest church in the State of Saxony.

Originally built in the late 14th century, it unfortunately has suffered numerous fires causing substantial rebuilding. In the 16th century, much of this church was restored in the Renaissance Style. The history of this church is marred by numerous fires and damage from wars such as being the target of cannons during the Seven Year's War. The near total destruction during WWII was just one of many unfortunate events in the life of this church.

Today, you may visit the interior of the church. While stark with minimal ornamentation, a feature common in many Lutheran churches, it is still very impressive. The balconies rise several levels above you.

The structure of the interior lends to incredible acoustics. If you are lucky, a concert will be happening while you are here. Check the website for details and schedule of events here. A noted boys choir, the Dresdner Kreuzchor boys choir, is based here.

Location: Just a few feet southeast from the Altmarkt Plaza and only a 7- or 8-minute walk south from the Neumarkt Plaza.

Website: www.Kreuzkirche-Dresden.de

12 – Shopping Street & Area – Prager Straße / Strasse:

This one-kilometer-long stretch (a bit over ½ mile) is one of two suggested shopping destinations in Dresden. The other locale, the Altmarkt-Galerie is adjacent to the northern end of Prager Straße. This busy, and very modern area has the Altmarkt Plaza as the northern point and Dresden's main train station, the Dresden Hbf at the southern end.

Prager Straße Shopping Street

Many Shops are Closed on Sunday

As a caution, Sunday is not a good time to go shopping here. In addition, several shops also close on Monday.

This is a shopper's heaven and is largely car free. Come here for boutiques and even another large mall, the Centrum Galerie. In addition to shops, numerous hotels also line the street and given the proximity to the train station, this is another great area to consider booking lodging.

5: New Town Points of Interest

Across the river from the historic center and on the "right bank" of Dresden, is another area to consider exploring. For most of us, this part of town should be explored only after visiting the Old Town.

In New Town, this is a more of a suburban feel with a mixture of apartment blocks, markets, dining, parks, office buildings, and, yes, a few notable attractions. The attractions are spread out, but the good news is that almost all of them are reachable by either the tram network or by taking the Hop-On Bus. (See chapter 7 for information on the Hop-On Bus system.

Dresden New Town / Neustadt Points of Interest List		
Map #[18]	Name	Type
13	Golden Rider	Statue of Agustus the Strong
14	Japanese Palace	Museums-Multiple
15	Neustadt Markthalle	Market Hall
16	Pfunds	Ornate Dairy & Cheese Shop

---

[18] **Map & Attraction Reference Numbers:** These start with #13, which can be a bit confusing, but this is a continuation of the numbered list in the previous chapter which focused on the heart of Dresden's Old Town.

A Starting-Point Guide

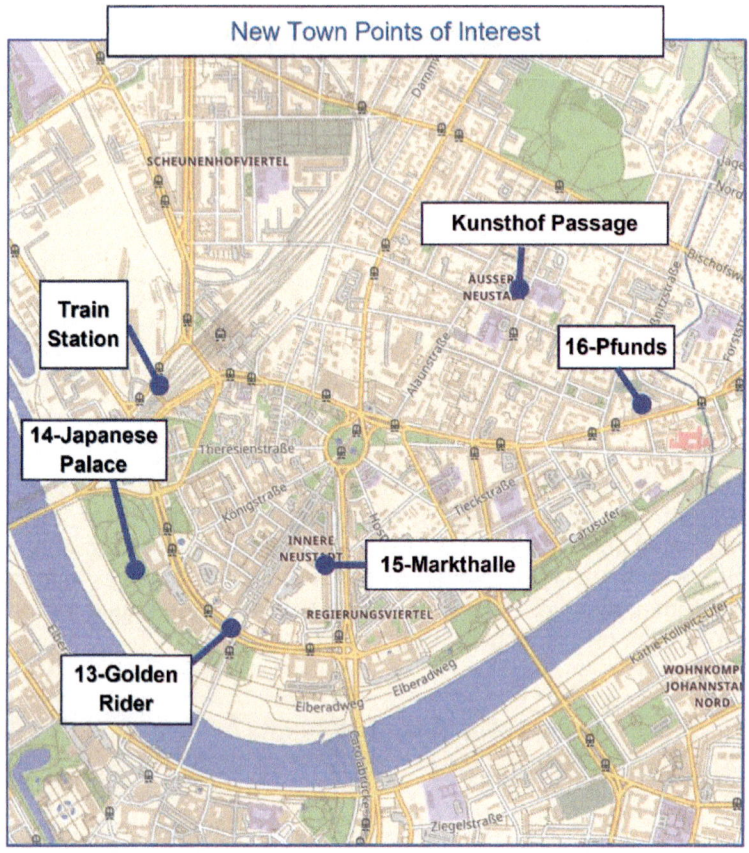

13 – Golden Rider Statue / Goldener Reiter:[19] A statue in gold leaf, dedicated to the former King of Saxony, Augustus the Strong, sits proudly in a small park near the entrance to New Town. Augustus is often given credit for crafting Dresden into an enjoyable and beautiful city. The statue was put here in his honor in 1736. This statue is often used as a symbol of the city.

---

[19] **Golden Rider Statue Name**: This is also commonly referred to as the Golden Horseman statue.

New Town Points of Interest

This small plaza and statue make a good starting point for exploring the riverfront and shopping opportunities near here. If you walk here from Old Town, you will be rewarded with an enjoyable stroll over the Elbe River. It is, depending on your starting point, less than a 10-minute stroll to get here.

What is Near Here:

- Great areas to take photos of the city from across the river. This is one of the better vantage points for great shots of the city. One of these is the "Canaletto-Blick", a strategically placed frame which enables you to include a frame around the city skyline in your photos.

- Public Restrooms – always an important feature.

- A long, tree-line shopping lane – the Haupstraße. This multi-block lane has some excellent restaurants. There is also a small "Museum of Dresden" here.

Golden Rider Statue
Photo Source: Jörg Blobelt-Wikimedia Commons

Transportation to here: Tram lines do stop right in front of the statue and plaza. The Hop-On Bus route does NOT stop here.

~ ~ ~ ~ ~

A Starting-Point Guide

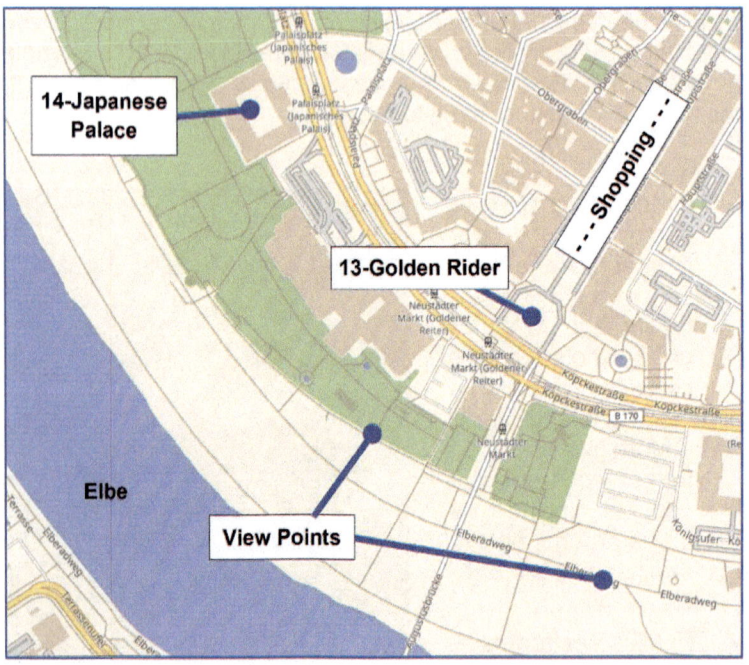

14 – Japanese Palace & Multiple Museums: The name of this museum building can be misleading. It was not a palace for anyone from Japan. It was built in 1715 to house the large collection of porcelains from Japan which had been acquired by Augustus the Strong. Today, that porcelain collection is part of the extensive porcelain museum in the Zwinger Palace complex across the river.

This building now houses three museums:
- Museum of Natural History
- Museum of Ethnology
- State Museum of Pre-History

New Town Points of Interest

Dresden's Japanese Palace & Natural History Museum
Photo Source: Jörg Blobelt - Wikimedia Commons

How To Get Here: This is best reached by the tram system (see Chapter 7 for more details on local transportation). If you choose to walk here from Old Town, expect a trek of about 15 minutes. The Hop-On Bus does not stop here.

What is Here: In addition to the three museums (all have free admission), consider taking some time, if it is a nice day, to roam the large gardens. Also, the riverfront has a lengthy bike and walking path. This route is a great area to get photos of the city across the river. The Golden Rider monument and adjacent shopping area is only a 6-to-8-minute walk away.

Hours: Open every day except Monday from 10AM to 6PM. Like most area museums, this is closed on Monday.

Website: Japanisches-Palais.Skd.Museum

~ ~ ~ ~ ~

15 – Neustadt Market Hall / Markethalle: An interesting activity for many of us is visiting local markets, such as farmers markets. Doing this is a great way to learn about local food products, wines, specialty dishes, and even gift items.

Neustadt Market Hall
Photo Source: VSchagow - Wikimedia Commons

In Dresden, there is a good market in the Neustadt area to explore. It is not huge, but the vendors provide a cross section of the area's gourmet and gift opportunities. A highlight of visiting here is the building itself. It first opened in 1899 and the interior is made largely of iron with several ornamental railings and staircases.

Location: The address is: Metzer Strasse 1, Dresden. It is easy to miss as it is tucked back slightly from the main shopping lane of Haupstraße. This neighboring Haupstraße, is a popular destination and is lined with many shops and restaurants. Coupling a visit to the Market Hall and this shopping district is a good mixture. This is only a five-minute walk from the Golden Rider Statue.

Hours: Closed on Sunday – most other days it is open from 8AM to 8PM. Mornings are best for the fresh produce.

Website: www.Markthalle-Dresden.de

16 – Pfunds Dairy Store / Dresdner Molkerei Gebrüder Pfund:
This place is fun and the word ornate barely begins to describe it. First, a bit about the identifier of "Dairy Store." Probably a better descriptor would be to call this a Cheese Shop. However, it doesn't stop there as you can find anything from cosmetics to jams and, yes, cheese. Oh, and there is also a small café here as well.

Pfunds Dairy Store Interior
Photo Source: Jörg Blobelt - Wikimedia Commons

Products aside, what makes this 140+ year old store special is the interior. It is now one of Dresden's most unique shopping destinations. The store's tilework is stunning with the walls and ceilings lined with Villeroy and Boch tiles.

Be prepared to find crowds as this is a stop for many tour groups and it is also a stop for the Hop-On Bus. Curiously, given the ornate interior, if you didn't

Pfunds was cited as the

"World's Most Beautiful Dairy Shop"

by the Guiness Book of Records.

know this store was a special place to visit, it would be easy to just drive or walk by. The street it is on and the front of the building are rather nondescript.

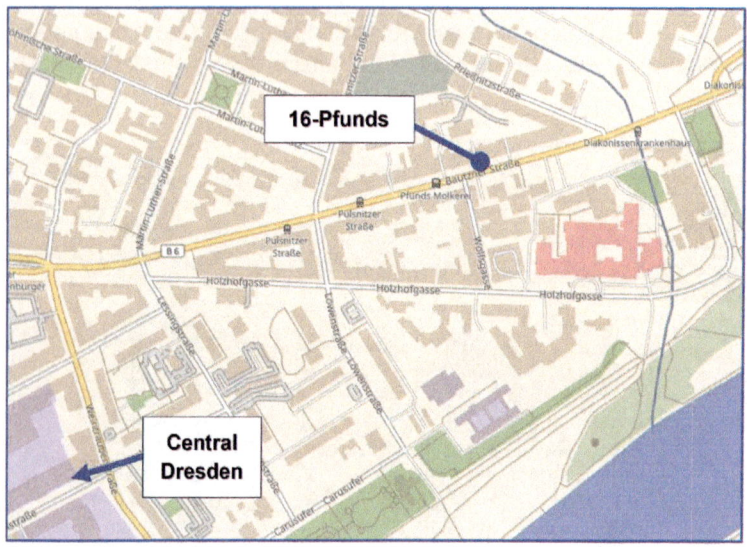

Fees: This is a store and not a formal attraction, so there is no entry fee. Do come with an open wallet as the wares are appealing.

Address & Getting Here: The location is such that few of us will choose to walk here. It is a bit over 2 kilometers northeast from the Golden Rider Statue and the address is Bautzner Strasse 79, Dresden. This store is reachable by tram or bus. Travel to the Pulsnitzer Straße stop which is a few doors down from Pfunds.

Hours: Closed on Sunday. All other days the store opens at 10AM and closes at either 5 or 6 PM depending on the day.

Website: www.Pfunds.de. This site includes information on the café along with an online store.

6: Attractions A Bit Further Out

Not all of Dresden's noteworthy sights are in the heart of the Old Town or New Town. A few of the popular destinations, such as a palace, are a short distance away and generally are not within an easy walk. The good news is that all of these locations are reachable by the tram system and/or the Hop-On Bus routes, so hiring a cab or renting a car is not needed.

Attractions Close to Old Town and New Town		
Map #[20]	Name	Type
Right Bank		
17	Military History Museum	German Military History
18	Schloss Albrechtsberg	Palace
19	Loschwitz	Funiculars
Left Bank		
20	Hygiene Museum	German Hygiene Museum
21	Grosser Garten	Large Park with palace
22	Dresden Zoo	Zoo
23	Panometer	Multi-Media Experience

---

[20] **Map Reference Numbers:** These start with #17. This is a continuation of the numbered list in the previous chapters which focused on Dresden's Old Town and New Town areas.

17 – Bundeswehr Museum of Military History: Sitting slightly north from the heart of Neustadt is a large museum dedicated to the history of Germany's armed forces. The building itself is a former military structure, an arsenal.

This is a relatively new museum as it was just opened in 2011. It is not a museum which simply focuses on or glamorizes the military. While there are many intriguing displays of armaments throughout Germany's history, an underlying theme is on war itself, its causes, and impacts.

Attractions A Bit Further Out

Military History Museum

Location and Getting Here: The address is Olbrichtpl 2, Dresden. It is tucked off from the main street, so it is easy to miss. The distance is almost 2.5 km north of the river (around 1.5 miles) so taking public transportation is suggested. The tram stop is Dresden Stauffenbergallee. This museum is NOT a stop on the Hop-On bus route.

Hours: Open every day except Wednesday. Typical hours are from 10AM to 6 PM.

Facilities: Note, as of this writing, there is no café on site and there are very few restaurants close by.

Website: www.Mmmbw.de

Palaces Near Central Dresden: The Saxony region has hundreds of palaces and castles, so you don't have to go far to find some noteworthy palaces to explore. Of the three beautiful palaces very close to central Dresden and overlooking the Elbe River, only one of them, Schloss Albrechtsberg, is open for tours.

Two other palaces are next to Schloss Albrechtrsberg but are not recommended as of this writing as they are not tour oriented.

- LingnerSchloss – A beautiful riverfront palace, but it does not offer tours. There is a restaurant and beer garden on site – for details, check their website at: www.LingerSchloss.de
- Schloss Eckberg – Another beautiful riverfront palace but it does not offer tours. This property is now functioning as a hotel which could be an interesting experience, but it is not recommended for casual visits and touring. For details, check www.Schloss-Eckberg.de

Also, see Chapter 10 for some guidance on notable, and easily reachable, castle day trips from Dresden.

18 – Schloss Albrechtsberg: Of the three palaces which sit in a row facing the river, this one tends to provide the best overall experience. This is a bit east of the heart of Dresden, so use of local transportation will be needed.

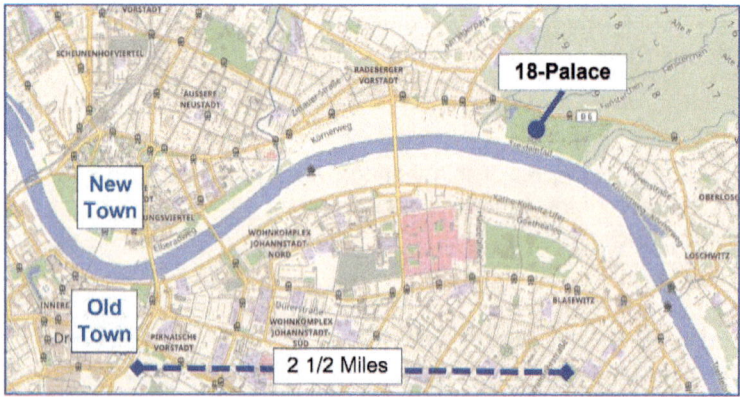

Schloss Albrechtsberg was built in 1854 and sits on a bluff overlooking the Elbe River. It was built for a former prince of Prussia who had left Prussia due to a marriage which had put him in disfavor. It was lived in by various family members up until 1925.

Unfortunately, the reason for the family selling off the property was because of huge gambling debts. Since then, it has served a variety of purposes ranging from a children's home to a residence for members of Russia's Red Army.

Schloss Albrechtsberg

Today, this palace (often referred to as a castle) is used for a variety of functions including a catering school and as a wedding venue. If you have deep pockets, you may even rent out the entire property for a special event.

Tours: Guided tours are available but somewhat limited in availability, so advanced booking via their website is recommended. The tours take one hour. Note, just dropping in and hoping to be able to tour the castle is not advised.

Getting Here: The Hop-On Bus Route does come here as well as the tram system – get off at the Elbschlosser stop. If you have rented a bicycle, it is an easy and scenic ride to here.

Website: www.Schloss-Albrechtsberg.de

19 – Loschwitz Cable Car & Funicular: The village of Loschwitz, which is about 3 miles east of central Dresden, has two very different funiculars. Each works their way up from near the river and each of them takes you to viewpoints on the bluffs overlooking the river. What differs, and in a fun way, is the nature of the ride. It is also helpful that the base stations for each of these funiculars are less than a five-minute walk from each other and that walk is through an attractive village.

> The Hop-On Bus stops here.

Advanced ticket purchase is not needed. Details on both systems may be found at www.DVB.de

Dresden Suspension Railway / Schwebebahn Dresden: This short ride up 276 feet (84 meters) in elevation is on a funicular which hangs from the rails above. This is a steep and fun ride up to an area above the village of Loschwitz. Once you are at the top, there is a café and observation deck. There is little else to see here as the top station is in a residential area.

This unique funicular first opened in 1901 and has been operating for over 120 years. The total length of the ride is just 899 feet (274 meters) so, it is a short jaunt.

Dresden Suspension Railway - the Schwebebahn

Attractions A Bit Further Out

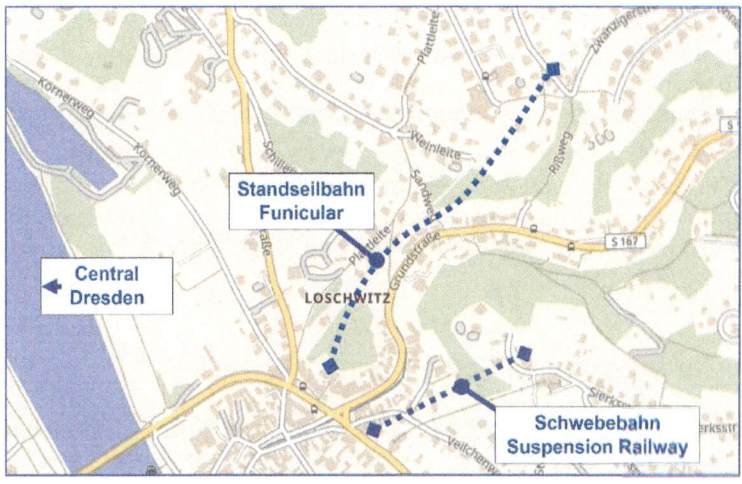

Dresden Funicular -Mountain Railway / Standseilbahn: This funicular, sometimes referred to as Dresden's Mountain Railway, is about twice the length of the neighboring suspension railway, but the total climb is only 30 feet more.

Dresden Funicular Railway - the Standseilbahn

This is a steep ride with an incline, at times, of 29%. Because of this, the cars have seats with each row sitting slightly higher than the downhill row of seats in front of it. This height staging provides for great views for most riders.

At the top, and directly across the lane from the station, is a German restaurant and beer garden, the Luisenhof, which offers great views of the river and city below. If you are lucky and the weather is favorable, consider having lunch here as the experience is top notch.

Left Bank Points of Interest:

Near Dresden's Old Town, and on the same side of the river, are several attractions which include a large city park, the zoo, and even a museum devoted to Hygiene. In all cases, they are easily reached by trams or buses. The walking distance to the heart of Old Town, depending on your starting point, will typically be around 20 to 30 minutes.

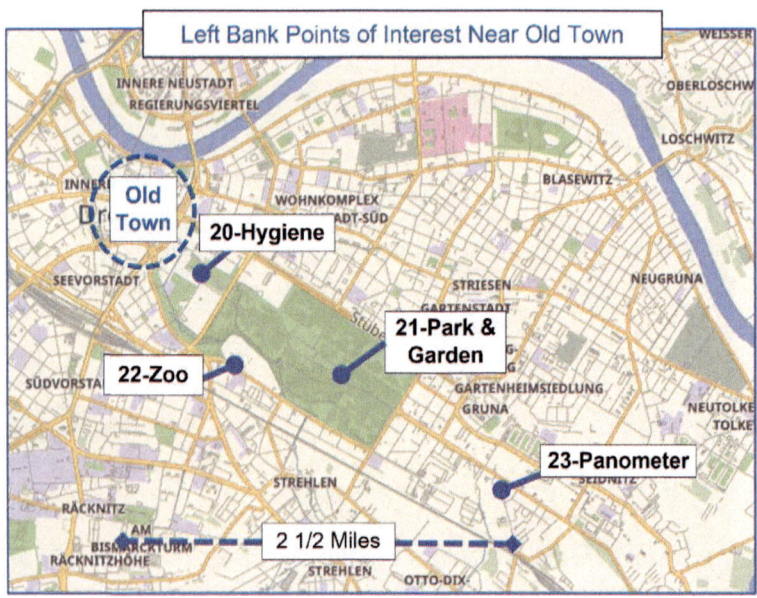

Attractions A Bit Further Out

Left Bank Points of Interest Near Old Town		
Map #	Name	Type
20	Hygiene Museum	German Hygiene Museum
21	Grosser Garten	Large Park with palace
22	Dresden Zoo	Zoo
23	Panometer	Multi-Media Experience

20 – Hygiene Museum / Deutsches Hygiene-Museum:
The museum's name really does not do a good job of stating its mission. This is a museum about science, society, and culture as it pertains to our bodies, not simply hygiene. It was started as something of a promotional tool in 1912 by a wealthy hygiene

Dresden Hygiene Museum
Photo Source: Raimond Spekking - Wikipedia

products manufacturer with the intent to promote healthcare education.

For many of us, spending part of a day going to a hygiene museum would not be at the top of the list. Therefore, it can come as a bit of a surprise to learn that this museum is very popular with almost 300,000 visitors each year. So, don't fear that you will be roaming empty hallways looking at toothbrushes by yourself.

Exhibits focus on humans, our bodies, senses, and health and much of this is placed into cultural contexts. Displays cover how different cultures approach differing topics ranging from psychology to reproduction and even climatic impacts.

Location: Lingnerplatz 1, Dresden. This is about a 15-minute walk east from the heart of Dresden's Prager Straße shopping area and about the same walking time to the zoo. Trams do not stop here.

Hours: Closed on Monday. Most other days, open from 10AM to 6PM.

Website: www.DHMD.de

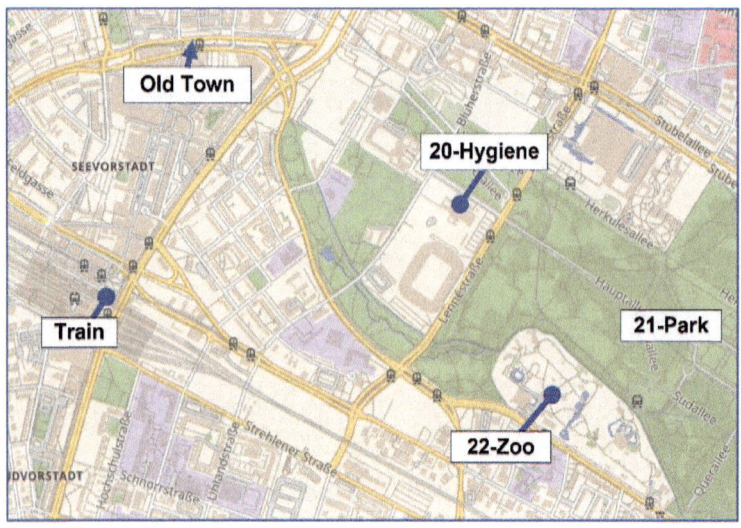

21 – Grand Garden Park / Großer Garten: This is Dresden's largest park and often considered to be its most appealing. There is a bit of everything here and it is a wonderful escape from the buzz of the city.

Grand Garden Park / Großen Gartens
Photo Source: Patrick Ribeiro - Wikipedia

Look for this by various names including Grosser Garden, Groß en Gartens, and Grand Garden. In size, it covers over 360 acres (147 hectares) so, there is plenty of room to roam. Inside the park, you will find:

- Botanical Garden
- Dresden Park Railway – a fun trip for families.
- The Zoo
- The Grand Garden Palace – a 17th century Baroque masterpiece.
- Outdoor cafe
- Numerous ponds and trails.

Tram Stop: Tram lines stop along both the northern and southern sides of the park.

Website: www.Grosser-Garten-Dresden.de

22 – Dresden Zoo: This is one of Germany's oldest zoos, having opened in 1861. It is a part of the large Grand Garden Park (Großen Park) making it easy to combine a visit to the zoo and park.

Although this is a modest-size zoo (23 hectares / 56 acres), it houses roughly 1000 animals across 200 species. A highlight is the Asian area. Features include an Africa house, monkey house, and walk-in aviaries. For children, several playgrounds are located throughout the property. There is also a café.

Fees: As of mid-2024, the adult fare is 15 Euro or 7 Euro for children. Rates are lower on Monday's. If you have a Dresden City Card (See Chapter 8), the rates are about half of the full rate.

Hours: Open times are typically from 8:30AM to 5:30PM. It does stay open until 6:30PM during the Spring to Fall period.

Website: www.Zoo-Dresden.de

Dresden Zoo - Adjacent to Großen Park
Photo Source: Wakowik - Wikipedia

~ ~ ~ ~ ~

Attractions A Bit Further Out

23 – Panometer: Located a short tram ride east from the park is an unusual artistic display. The Dresden Panometer sits in a round building which once was a large gas storage tank. Now, it is one large circular gallery with two panoramic paintings of Dresden. One work depicts the city in 1756, the other shows the city right after its near complete destruction in WWII. Each of the panoramas is nearly 90 feet tall and over 300 feet around.

Dresden Panometer
Photo Source: asisi F & E- Wikipedia

Location: Gasanstaltstraße 8B, Dresden. This is a bit over one kilometer east from the park and in something of an industrial area. Neither the Hop-On Buses nor trams stop here but you may take a bus to the Dresden Nätherstraße stop.

When Open: Open every day. Typical hours are from 10AM to 5PM.

Website: www.Panometer-Dresden.de

7: Getting Around in Dresden
Hop-On Bus, Trams & Bicycles

When visiting Dresden, a majority of the historic sights are in one fairly small area, so transportation issues are not likely to be an issue. If, however, you will be here for more than one or two days, learning how to navigate the city's transportation options can be beneficial. Consider downloading one of the many apps, such as the GPS My City Map and Walks App. Apps such as these provide suggested walks based on your interests. Details on most attractions and even restaurants will be included.

> The Dresden Map and Walks App is a good resource to help you navigate the city on foot.

Hop-On/Hop-Off Bus Tour / The Stadtrundfahrt: Hop-On/Hop-Off bus tours can be found in most cities which attract tourism and Dresden is no exception. It is easy to think of this service as excessively touristy, but these bus tours do offer several benefits. In addition to taking you to the expected and most popular attractions close to the city center, these services provide a good feel for a city and often take you to and through neighborhoods which you would have missed. When taking these tours, you will almost always come away with a good overall feel for the city and not just the tourist-centric center.

In Dresden, the service covers over 20 stops, and the route takes about two hours, if you do not get off at any point. About half of the stops are clustered around Dresden's Old Town with a couple in New Town. Probably the biggest plus to the route are the several stops to the east of town which take riders to the funiculars and palaces described in the previous chapter.

Dresden Hop-On / Hop-Off Bus Tour
Photo Source: www.Stadtrundfahrt.de

Some Details:
- You may start your route at any point. The official starting point is next to Zwinger palace.
- Headphones are provided in several languages.
- The frequency of bus tours differs by the season. During the high season from April to October, buses run every 15 to 30 minutes, so if you choose to get off along the route, you do not have to wait long for the next bus. During the Nov to March season, it can be as long as one hour between buses, so take care when you hop off.
- Numerous ticket and tour package options are available such as combining the bus tour with a funicular ride so checking the website for options in advance can be helpful. One good option is tickets which cover 24 hours of travel.

Website: www.Stadtrundfahrt.de

Trams & Buses:[21] Dresden has a combination of tram lines and buses which enable easy transit throughout the metropolitan area. The one downside is that, due to its extensive nature, it can take a bit to figure out which route is best to take.

There are several tram lines and stops which service Dresden's Old Town.

The tram network is extensive and is a combination of street-level trams and light rail. In total, there are twelve different lines which span 210 kilometers (Over 130 miles). This large number of lines does mean there is some learning curve when you first use the system.

> **Tram and Bus App**
> Consider downloading the DVB Mobil app. This is an excellent aid for using this system.

---

[21] **Tram and Bus Customer Service Center:** In Dresden, there is an office on the busy Postplatz street. The office is very close to the Altmarkt-Galerie shopping center and only a short distance from the heart of Old Town. If you need any help, tickets, or maps, consider stopping in here. The address is: Postplatz 1. It is easy to find.

Getting Around in Dresden

Luckily, there are great apps which will give you details on the lines and stops you need for your intended travel.

> **Dresden Welcome Card / City Card**
> These cards include the local transportation system so no additional passes are needed. See Chapter 8 for further information.

Ticket Options: In addition to simply purchasing a ticket for a single ride, there are passes available specifically for tourists and short-term visitors. The availability of these passes somewhat eases the complexity of deciding which ticket or pass to purchase.

If you purchase a one-day pass, this is NOT a 24-hour pass, it is only good for the day you purchase the ticket and until 4AM the next morning. Do not purchase a pass thinking you can first use it late in the day and have the pass still be valid until the same time the next day.

Tickets may be purchased from machines on every Tram car or at every tram stop.
Photo Source: www.DVB.de

Most ticket and pass options may be purchased from: the website at www.DVB.de,[22] the DVB app, any of the ticket machines which are found at most tram and bus stops, and from ticket machines directly on board each tram.

---

[22] **Transportation Company in Dresden**: the DVB system (www.DVB.de) manages the trams, buses, the funiculars, and even the local bike-share service.

Pass Types to Consider: [23]

- One-Day Pass – sold on a per-person basis. There are 4 "zone" variations which can be confusing. If most of your travel will be in Old Town and New Town, all you need is a 1 fare zone. Beyond this, it is best to check the fare zone map which is posted on the website and at most tram stops.

> **Senior Citizen and Child Discounts**
> All pass types are available at a slight discount for: (1) Senior Citizens over 60 years old, and (2) Children under 15 years old.

- One-Day Family Pass. This covers two adults and up to four children under the age of 15. There are three zone price options available. As with the One-Day Pass, you will likely only need the lower cost one-fare zone pass if your travels are limited to Old Town and New Town.

- Small Group Ticket: Similar to the family pass but, the members of your group do not need to include children or family members. This covers up to five people and there are three fare zone options.

---

[23] **Ticket Prices:** This guide does not cite specific ticket or pass prices simply because prices do change. As of mid-2024 and as a general guideline, expect to pay between 7 € to 15€ per person per day, depending on the pass you select.

Bicycle Rental: Much of Dresden can easily be explored on bicycle and with most of the metropolitan area on flat land, it is easy to find an enjoyable and relaxing route.

There are several firms which provide bicycle and e-bike rentals. By far, the largest service is Mobi Bike with over 60 self-serve stations and more than 1,300 rental bikes throughout the city.

To rent a bicycle from this service, either use the app or the rental kiosk at each station. Bikes may be returned to any station with available docking slots. The app will indicate if bikes are available to rent and, when you are ready to return, which stations have open slots to return your bike.

> Mobi bike / Next Bike
>
> This service, while offered under the auspices of Dresden's DVB transportation network, is actually provided by Next Bike. This firm provides bicycle rental in hundreds of cities and once you have set up an account with them, and download the Nextbike app, you are set for bicycle rental everywhere it is offered

There are several available rates. A one-day rental will be roughly 15 Euro and bikes may be rented for any period desired.

Website: www.NextBike.de/Dresden - or visit the transportation website at www.DVB.com.

8: City & Area Passes and Tours

If you will be staying in Dresden for several days and participating in multiple activities or tours in this city, consider purchasing one of the available discount cards. Multiple programs are offered with the two leading cards being provided by the Dresden tourist office.

The existence of very similar programs, the **Dresden City Card** and the **Dresden Regio Card**, can lead to some confusion. In actuality, the key difference is the geography covered. [24]

- Dresden City Card – the focus is on attractions and transportation in the city.

- Dresden Regio Card – similar types of attractions and transportation are covered, but for a larger geographical area.

> Recommendation
>
> **The Dresden City Card**
>
> For most of us, this card is all that is needed. There is not enough extra in where the Regio Card can be used to justify the large price increase… unless you will be making several trips via the tram and light rail system outside of central Dresden.

---

[24] **Detailed Discount Card Comparison**: For a list of attractions and discounts included in each program, visit www.Dresden.de then click on the "Tourism" link.

City Passes and Tours

What is Included in the Two Programs:

- **Local Transportation:** Unlimited travel on local trams and buses. The City Card includes just travel in and close to the city center while the Regio Card covers the entire metro area.
- **Discounts:** Both cards offer discounts on numerous area tours, restaurants, and attractions. A small number of attractions will have free entrance with these cards. The Regio Card includes a few more sites which provide discounts. Each of these are outside of central Dresden.

Costs: Both the Welcome Card and Regio Card are available for 1 day, 2 days, or 3 days. Also, both cards offer the two variations of individual tickets or Family Tickets. The Family passes cover two adults and up to four children under fifteen.

Welcome Card and Regio Card Cost Comparison[25]				
	Single Passes		**Family Passes**	
Duration	**City Card**	**Regio Card**	**City Card**	**Regio Card**
1 Day	€ 17	€ 26	€ 21	€ 40
2 Days	€ 24	€ 44	€ 35	€ 60
3 Days	€ 33	€ 59	€ 45	€ 84

---

[25] **Card Price Note and Caution:** The rates cited here are as of mid-2024 and are subject to change. Use this chart as a general guideline only.

Where to Buy: While several online services do resell these passes, it is generally best to buy directly from the provider. In this case, it is the Dresden tourist office at: www.Dresden.de. These passes may be purchased in advance online or when you are in town. Their office is in the heart of Old Town adjacent to the Neumarkt Plaza.

The SchlosserlandCard: In addition to the Welcome Card and Regio Card cited on the previous pages, another pass type is available. The Schlosserland Card covers most of Saxony and does provide admission to attractions not included in the Welcome Card such as the Festung Xperience. This card also covers several area castles and palaces.

The shortest duration for this card is 10 days. It is not intended for visitors who are here for a short stay.

This is a good card to consider IF you will be in the area for over a week and much of your exploring will be outside of central Dresden.

Full details on this card may be found at: www.Schlosserland-Sachsen.de. Look for the link to the discount card.

Dresden Tour Companies: If your schedule allows, consider taking one of the many tours within Dresden. These tours range from short 1- or 2-hour events to full day explorations.

Even if you are disinclined to join structured group events, at least one tour should be considered as they almost always enhance your understanding of the city, its history, and main attractions.

Most tours of interest will be available from the Tourist Office, and many may be purchased in advance.

Numerous online services enable you to explore available tours and purchase passes. These offerings often go well beyond those offered by the Tourist Office and some tours may be customized to your specifications.

Some of the leading tour providers are:[26]

- www.Dresden.de – Dresden Tourist Office
- TripAdvisor.com – Search for Dresden and go to the tours page.
- Viator.com - A service of Trip Advisor
- GetYourGuide.com – Search for Dresden to view the provided tours.
- ToursByLocals.com - This firm offers many private and small-group tours.

Example Dresden City Tours: Following is a list of several recommended tours. Each of these may be purchased from the Dresden Tourist Office. Many other tours are available through other companies such as those cited above. The Tourist Office is a great place to start your search for tours as they offer

---

[26] **Tour Providers Note:** The five providers cited here are a representative listing only and this is not intended to be a comprehensive list of firms which provide tour services in the area.

a full variety ranging from walking, historic, gastronomic, historical, and even whimsical tour offerings.

- Hop-On Bus Tours – The Tourist Office provides several packages which include the Hop-On Buses plus add-ons such as boat tours or funicular rides.

- Neustadt Walking Tour – 90-minute walking tour of some of the trendy areas of Neustadt (the area across the river from Old Town Dresden).

- Old Town Tour – A three-hour comprehensive walking tour of the Old Town, taking you to several of the more notable buildings such as the Semperoper Dresden Opera House.

- Boat Tour along the Elbe - A 90-minute boat tour which provides great views of the city. Fun experience on a warm day.

- Dresden Culinary Tour – Two and a half hour walking tour with an experienced guide taking you to some of the hidden culinary treasures including local wines.

- Saxony Area Tours – Several offerings are available, most are full day, which take you into the nearby country including palace visits.

The above list is only a small sample of available tours which will help you become acquainted with Dresden. All of the above are provided by the Tourist Office, but similar offerings may be found from other leading tour providers such as Viator, Get Your Guide, and others.

If you are seeking enjoyable day trip destinations, such as a trip to the historic town of Meissen or to the Saxon Switzerland National Park, Chapter 10 provides more detail on these opportunities.

9: Where to Stay in Dresden

Quality lodging may be found throughout Dresden but, determining where to stay as a first-time visitor need not be complicated. This guide outlines two neighboring areas to consider booking your lodging. These two "areas" are essentially subsets of Dresden's Altstadt or Old Town. In each case, these sections of town provide easy access to main sights, transportation, shopping, and dining.

Other areas are not detailed here simply because they are not as central to the Old Town region of town. An alternative to the two suggested areas in this guide is in Neustadt, across the river. This is a good area for dining. Travel into Old Town is not difficult, but no hotels are cited here because of the overall reduction in convenience when compared to lodging in or close to Old Town. One positive aspect of New Town, however, is the room rates tend to be a bit less.

In addition, the focus of this guide is on hotels and not apartment rentals such as Air BnB. When considering lodging, using a source such as TripAdvisor.com or Booking.com is recommended as they can provide far more detail and up-to-date reviews.

Recommendation

Good news – there is a large area where you generally can't go wrong. This sector for lodging stretches from the Elbe River at the north, south almost all the way to the train station.

A Starting-Point Guide

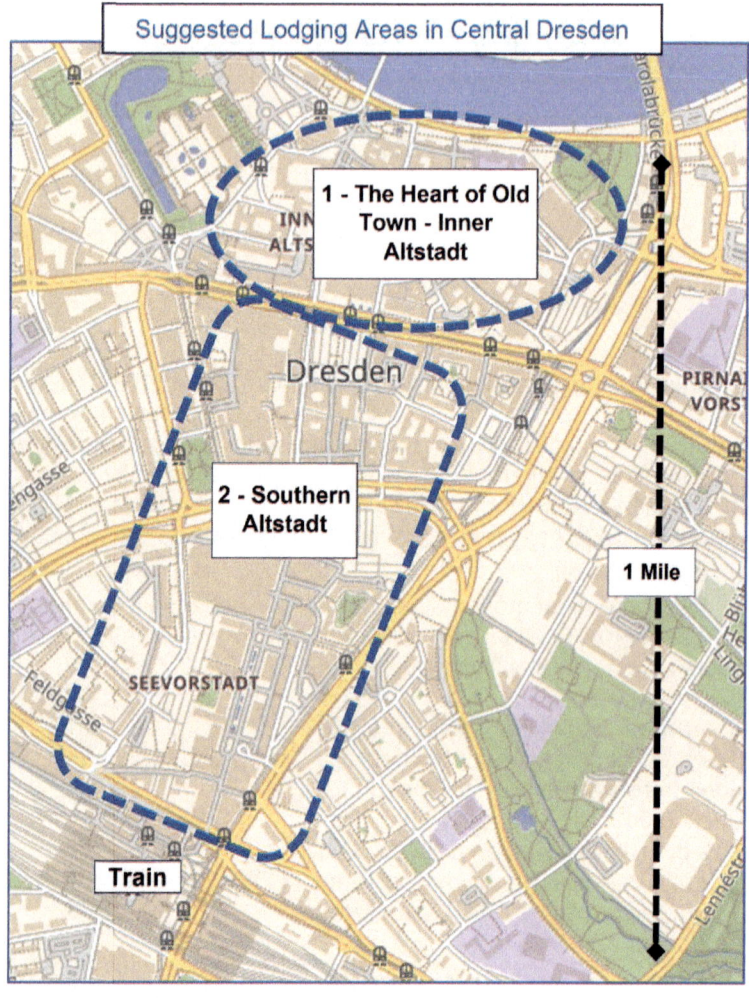

27

---

[27] **Southern Altstadt Name** – this term is not a formal designation. It is used in this chapter simply as a directional aid to help understand where this suggested area for lodging sits.

Central Old Town / Inner Altstadt: [28] This lodging is in the very center of the historic district with its numerous shops and restaurants. Some of the city's most luxurious hotels are here but, some budget properties can be found as well. The only downsides to staying here are (a) crowds from tourism and events, and (b) parking can be a bit far for some of these properties.

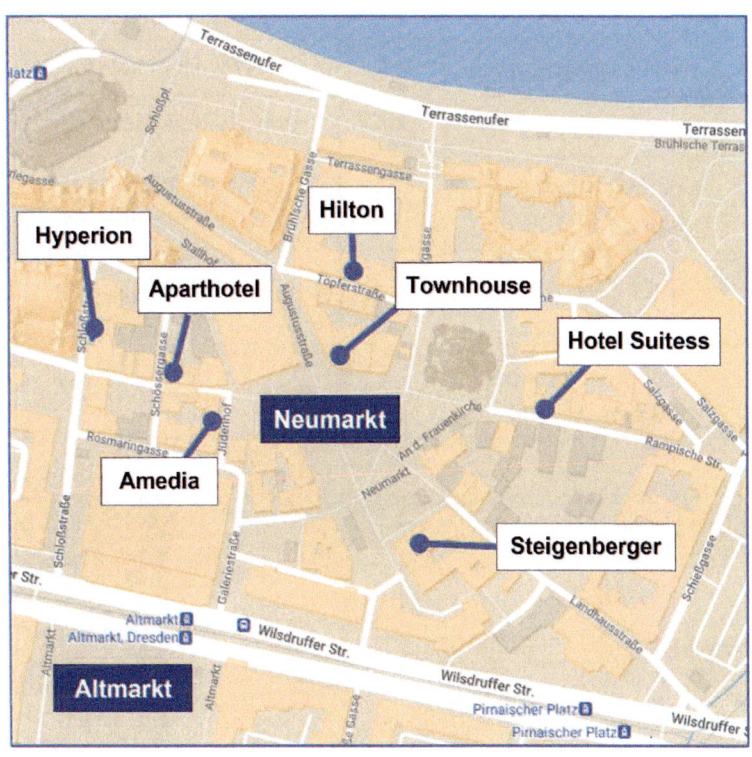

---

[28] **Lodging Ratings in this Guide:** All ratings depicted for hotels in this Starting-Point Guide are a mix of the author's opinion and blend of external rating sources. No one single source was used. As a bit of general advice, consider utilizing your favorite booking source such as Trip Advisor or Hotels.com to see how those services rate each property.

A Starting-Point Guide

Properties to consider in Dresden Old Town		
Hotel Name	Rating	Website
Amedia Plaza Dresden	4	www.WyndamHotels.com
Aparthotel Am Schloss	4	www.Aparthotels-Frauen-kirche.de
Hilton Dresden	4.5	www.Hilton.com
Hotel Suitess	4.5	www.Suitess-Hotel.com
Hyperion Hotel Dresden am Schloss	4.5	www.H-Hotels.com (Author favorite)
Steigenberger Hotel de Saxe	4.5	www.HRewards.com
Townhouse Dresden Vagabond Club	4	www.VagabondClub.com

The Dresden Hilton - one of several notable hotels in the heart of Old Town.
Photo Source: Jörg Bolbelt - Wikimedia Commons

Altmarkt and South to the Train Station: In the area which stretches south from central Old Town for roughly 2/3 of a mile (about 1 km) down to the train station, are numerous hotels and other lodging opportunities. This area is the focal point for Dresden's downtown/zentrum shopping including two notable shopping centers.

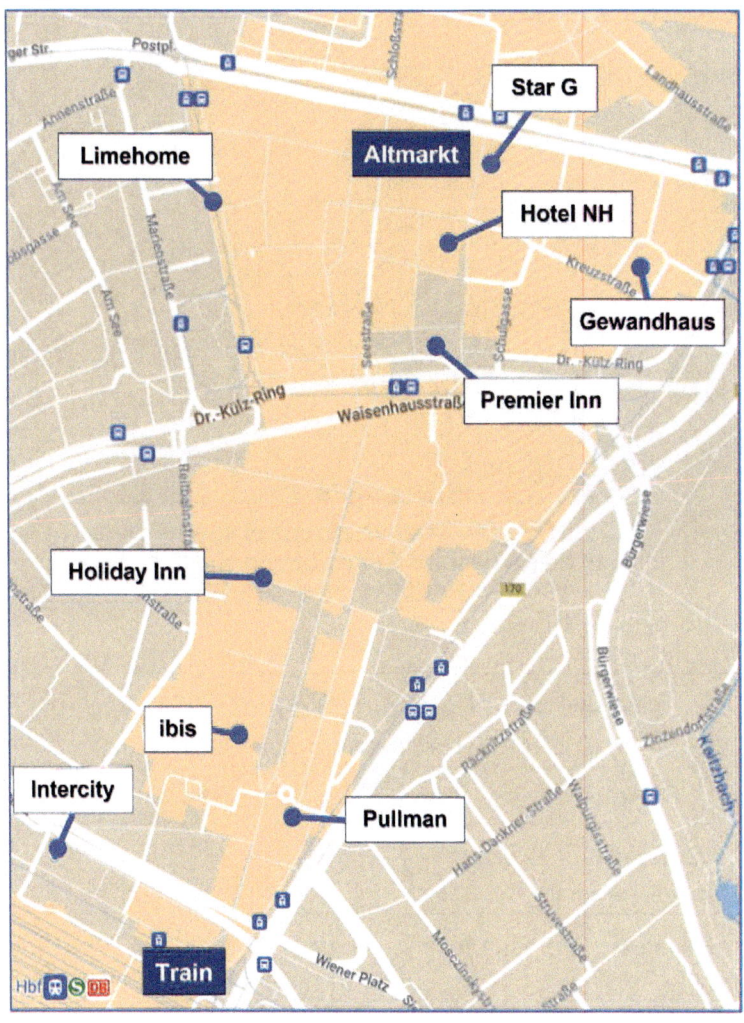

This area is very convenient not only for shopping but for the many restaurants which line areas such as Prager Straße. Also, if you are likely to take day trips by train, having the main train station nearby can be very helpful. Lodging here tends to be slightly less expensive than in the heart of the Old Town and many good quality hotels may be found here. Several of the city's largest hotels are here.

The ibis Dresden Zentrum - is one of several large, modern hotels near the Prager Straße shopping area.
Photo Source: ibis Hotels - Wikimedia Commons

Properties to Consider South of Old Town		
(Only properties with a 3.5 rating or better are included)		
Hotel Name	Rating	Website
Gewandhaus Dresden (Marriott Autograph Collection)	5	www.Marriott.com (Author favorite)
Holiday Inn Express Dresden	3.5	www.IHG.com (Quality on a budget)

Properties to Consider South of Old Town
(Only properties with a 3.5 rating or better are included)

Hotel Name	Rating	Website
Hotel NH Collection Dresden Altmarkt	4	www.nh-Hotels.com (Very close to Old Town)
Ibis Dresden Zentrum	3.5	www.ibis-Dresden.de (Huge, full-service hotel)
Intercity Hotel Dresden	4	www.hRewards.com (Convenient to train station)
Limehome Dresden Wallstraße	4	www.LimeHome.com (Small Apartments)
Premier Inn Dresden	4.5	www.PremierInn.com (Large and modern)
Pullman Hotel Dresden	4	www.Pullman-Hotel-Dresden.de (Large and modern)
Star G Hotel Premium Dresden Altmarkt	3.5	wwwStargGHotels.com (Close to Altmarkt)

10: Day Trips from Dresden
Castles – Natural Wonders – Quaint Towns

Several opportunities for enjoyable and informative day trips out of town are available. These trips range from touring numerous palaces and castles to visiting the beautiful Saxon Switzerland National Park.

Only destinations which are easy to reach by train or available tours are included. And only destinations which are less than 90 minutes away from central Dresden are outlined here. The goal is to enable you to have an easy day trip or half-day trip without wearing yourself down.

This chapter outlines seven destinations to consider. This is far from a complete list of enjoyable area locales, but they do provide a good cross-section of experiences

Day Trip Destinations Included in This Guide[29]		
Name	**Distance[30]**	**Type of Destination**
Bautzen	31 Miles 50 KM	Attractive small town with castle and cathedral.
Leipzig	63 Miles 101 KM	Interesting large town with many historic buildings.
Meissen	13 Miles 21 KM	Another attractive town. Porcelain factory and palace visits.
Moritzburg Palace[31]	9 Miles 14 KM	Expansive castle and grounds near Dresden.
Pillnitz Palace	7 Miles 11 KM	Palace complex and park close to Dresden.
Saxon Switzerland Park	16 Miles 26 KM	National Park with hiking trails and beautiful scenery.
Weesenstein Castle	10 Miles 16 KM	15th Century Castle

---

[29] **Destinations Listed Alphabetically:** The day trip destinations outlined here are organized alphabetically. This order does not suggest any sort of priority or importance in which destination to consider over others.

[30] **Distances Cited:** All distances listed in the table on this page are "as the crow flies" from central Dresden to the center of the destination site or area. Actual driving or train distances will likely be greater.

[31] **Palace or Castle?** Both terms are given to the various palaces and castles in the area, depending on which reference source you use. The author has defaulted to using the term shown on the website for each location.

Bautzen, Germany – The City of Towers: If you are looking for a quiet escape to a picturesque town which offers an appealing town center and several historic buildings including a castle and cathedral, consider heading to Bautzen. This is a small city which is not overrun with tourism, despite its charm. The population is roughly 37,000 people and is easy to reach by train from Dresden. This is, for most of us, a good half-day adventure. There is also a surprisingly large number of attractions to visit for a town this size.

Bautzen, Germany

Where to Start: In the heart of Bautzen is an attractive square, the Hauptmarkt. This is a good central point for any exploration of the town and there are several shops and restaurants here. The Tourist Office is here. All points of interest are within an easy stroll from this plaza.

Highlights: Your visit can be as simple as just strolling through this relaxing town or heading off to one of many interesting sights here. These include:

- Towers: Bautzen is often referred to as the City of Towers. There are 17 historic and greatly varying towers here including a leaning tower. Several of the towers are open to go up to the top for some great views of Bautzen and the area.

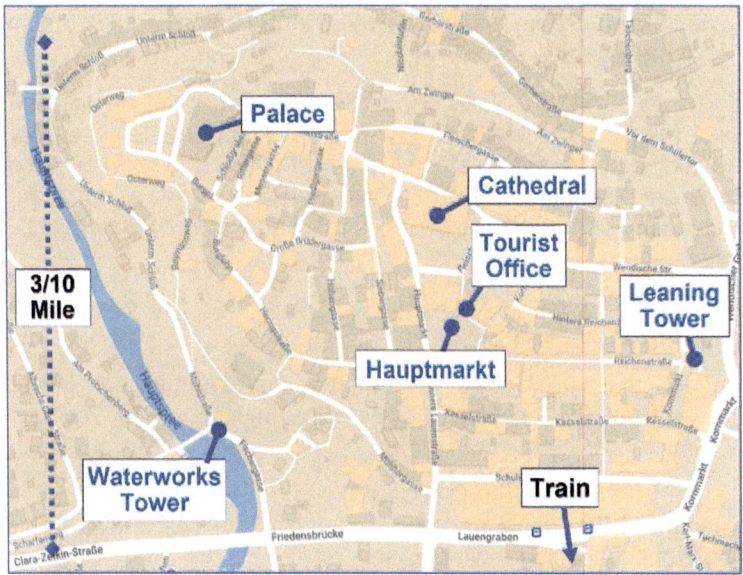

- Cathedral: The largest and most notable church here is the Cathedral of Saint Peter. This church dates back to the year 1000. One fascinating aspect of the church is it combines Catholic and Protestant religions. As a result, it is known as the "largest simultaneous church in Germany."
- Museums: Several museums are clustered in the heart of Bautzen. There are some interesting museums to consider here including one dedicated to Mustard and another focused on the local Sorbian culture.

Getting Here:
- Driving: This is about a 45-minute drive from central Dresden. Once you arrive in Bautzen, there is a large parking lot just one block north of the Hauptmarkt plaza.
- Train: Good news and bad news. Trains to Bautzen are frequent and most trains are direct and do not require a change.

The journey is typically about one hour. The downside is the station is about a half-mile south of central Bautzen. It is likely you may have to walk into town or, consider taking the bus into town. Route maps are posted at the bus stop just outside of the Bautzen station.

Tours to Bautzen: Take one of the available tours of Dresden for a relaxing and stress-free way to visit not only Bautzen but much of the area. There are only a few offerings and most of these tours are full-day and Bautzen will be just one stop along the route. Tour companies to check into for a journey to Bautzen include:

- Get Your Guide – www.GetYourGuide.com. Full day private tours. A bit expensive.

- Veronika's Adventure – www.VeronikasAdventure.com. Also, a private, full-day tour. They work in conjunction with Get Your Guide.

Bautzen Tourist Office: Located adjacent to the Hauptmarkt plaza. The website for this town and service is www.Bautzen.de. There is also an available app for Bautzen which provides details on the various tours and other sights.

> **Walking Tours**
>
> The Bautzen Tourist Office provides several walking tours and most focus on the history of this small city.

Leipzig, Germany – Saxony's Largest City:

Leipzig - Augustusplatz in the "Zentrum" of town.

This city of 600,000+ has enough to fill several days of exploring and it is not hard to have an enjoyable day trip from Dresden. If you focus on the city center (the "Zentrum"), you can come away with a good feel for this city without wearing yourself down.

Like Dresden, much of the city was destroyed during WWII and in shambles for several decades after the war. In recent decades, primarily since German reunification, the city has become a modern and thriving economic center. It has, in fact, grown faster than any other German city. Some of this growth can be attributed to the proximity to Berlin which was feeling growing pains and Leipzig was a natural "next best thing" for expansion.

When visiting here from Dresden, the contrast is significant. Yes, both cities have a mix of old and new and both cities have noteworthy history-rich destinations, but in Leipzig it simply feels different. Leipzig feels more vibrant and younger with the "new" feeling being more prominent than the "old." The presence of modern structures, along with major universities gives the city a young feel.

A Starting-Point Guide

This is an easy city to explore on foot for a one-day exploration. Even the train station (which is huge) is within steps of the heart of Leipzig – the Marktplatz, the city's main plaza.

<u>Where to Start:</u> Consider heading to either the Leipzig Tourist Information Office or the historic Marktplatz plaza to use as a starting point for your explorations. The Tourist Information

office[32] is in a popular shopping area roughly an 8-to-10-minute walk south of the train station. Then, two blocks south of here is a large and attractive plaza, the Marktplatz. There is another busy train station under this plaza.

> Leipzig Hop-On Bus
>
> If you wish to view more than the city center, consider using the city's Hop on Bus or City Tour Bus.
>
> Tickets are available from the Tourist Office or numerous online providers.

Highlights: For most of us, the primary interest will be to simply get a feel for this city and, if time allows poke into one of the notable museums or cathedrals. In Leipzig, you are in luck as most (not all) of the city's attractions are within a one-half mile square area, the "Zentrum." Another positive aspect of Leipzig's city center is that many of the lanes are pedestrian friendly with minimal traffic.

Shopping: It would be hard to miss the fact that central Leipzig is a shopping mecca. The shopping and browsing opportunities start with the train station (assuming that you come in by train). There is an expansive shopping and dining center in the lower level of the station.

Across the street and down a block from the train station is a three-story mall, the Höfe am Brühl. Then, the shopping just continues on southward to the Marktplatz and around the area.

Museums and Other Points of Interest: Not surprisingly, there are several museums in central Leipzig. There are several specialty museums such as one focusing on Egyptology and another on Vintage Culture. Among the most popular are:[33]

- Museum of Fine Arts – Easy to find, next to the Höfe am Brühl shopping center and the Tourist Information Office.

---

[32] **Leipzig Tourist Offices:** There are several locations in Leipzig, even one in the main train station. Full details on each location and the services they provide may be found on their website: www.Leipzig.Travel

[33] Leipzig Points of Interest: Please visit the Leipzig Tourist Office website for a complete list of points of interest.

- Bach Museum - The composer Bach lived here for 27 years. This museum is dedicated to his life and art.
- Stadtgeschichtliches Museum – Leipzig City and History Museum located in the old "Rathaus" next to the Marktplatz.

Observation Towers: There are several opportunities in central Leipzig to head to the top of one of the city's tall structures to see great views of the city. Among these are:
- City-Hochhaus – A modern skyscraper near the Augustusplatz in the southeastern quadrant of central Leipzig.
- St. Thomas Church – Take a tower tour up 223 feet. Caution, there are many steps involved.

Getting Here: Travel by train is recommended. It is quick, convenient, and you can avoid the hassles which come with driving into an unfamiliar and busy town. The main train station, Leipzig Hauptbahnhof, is immediately across the street from the heart of town. Train trips from Dresden are frequent and most take only a bit over one hour.

Tourist Office Website: There are multiple tourist-focused websites for Leipzig. The best one to use is www.Leipzig.travel. One great aspect of this site is the many downloadable brochures. This is also an excellent tour resource

Meissen, Germany – Porcelain & Imposing Castle: Just a few miles downriver (northwest) on the Elbe from Dresden is this town of 30,000. It provides an excellent complement to Dresden as the two are firmly linked historically and economically. Yes, there is a beautiful castle here which overlooks the river, but it is porcelain which provides the link between the two cities.

Meissen Porcelain was founded here by King Augustus the Strong in 1710. It was the first European porcelain manufacturer and has been a leader of decorative and artistic porcelain products ever since. Tours of the porcelain factory are available.

Meissen straddles the Elbe River but, the heart of town, most attractions, and the prominent Albrechtsburg castle are all on the left bank which make explorations fairly easy.

Meissen, Germany

Highlights: In addition to this being an appealing riverfront town that is easy to explore, the two main draws in Meissen are the imposing palace and Meissen Porcelain:

- Meissen Porcelain: Their museum, showroom, and shop are in the southwestern corner of town. This is roughly a 10-minute walk from the train station or a 15-minute walk into the heart of town. Tours of the factory or simply exploring their large museum will be impressive enough for most of us. For details, the website is: www.Meissen.com.
- Albrechtsburg Castle: A stunningly beautiful castle with a cathedral sitting on a low rise overlooking the town and river. Built in the late 15th century, this is the focal point of the town and where visitors will, and probably should go first. It is a bit of an uphill walk to here. For information on available tours, check: www.Albrechtsburg-meissen.de.

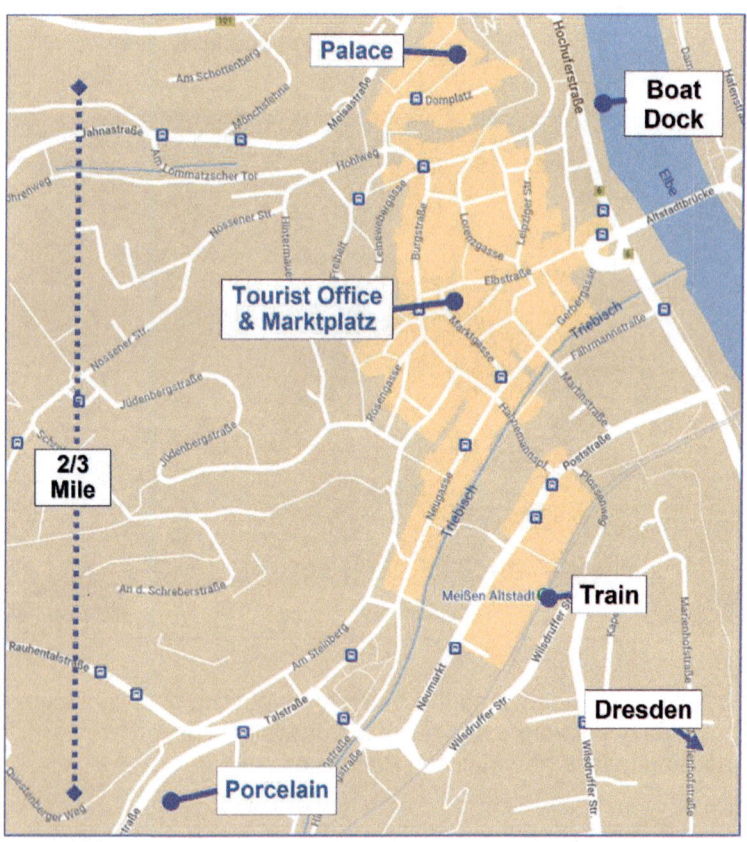

Getting Here:

- Train: There are two train stations so, when booking, be sure to select the Meissen/Meißen Altstadt station. This is not next to any major attractions, so a walk or bus ride once you arrive will be necessary. There is a bus stop close to the station. Trains run about every thirty minutes and the ride is less than forty minutes each way.

- Boat Tour: A truly enjoyable way to travel to Meissen from Dresden is via a boat tour. The ride each way takes about two hours, so you will need to plan for a full day to make the journey there and back. Several firms such as www.GetYourGuide.com offer this service. Once your boat arrives at Meissen, you have a short walk to the heart of town or up to the castle. Unfortunately, the porcelain factory and museum are a bit further out.

Tourist Office Website: The main tourist office is in central Meissen next to their Marktplatz, which is an attractive square with several restaurants and shops. Their website is: www.Stadt-Meissen.de

Moritzburg Castle / Schloss Moritzburg: When the Saxony empire was at its most powerful in the 16th century, it was en vogue for leaders to build impressive palaces and small castles, or simply your basic "Schloss". Moritzburg Castle is one of the region's more impressive and is open for visitors.

This is a Baroque-styled palace which was built in the 1540's for Duke "Moritz" as a hunting lodge. (They had a different concept of a hunting lodge back then.) The building didn't stop in the 16th century as later additions, such as a chapel, were added in the 17th and even the 18th centuries.

One of the visual strengths of this palace is the setting and its grounds. Adjacent to the palace is a formal park and lake. The lake even has a lighthouse. Not surprisingly, given the setting and the striking beauty of the palace, it has been used in several movies.

Moritzburg Castle / Schloss Moritzburg
Photo Source: Carsten Pietzsch - Wikipedia

Visiting the Palace: It is very close to the Dresden Airport north of town. This is open every day and visiting hours vary slightly by the season. To visit, you must purchase a ticket either online via the palace's website or at the entrance. Also, numerous tours out of Dresden include this palace in the area tours. Several tours combine Moritzburg with a visit to Meissen which was described on the previous pages. Check services such as www.ToursByLocals.com or www.GetYourGuide.com.

Getting Here: The best way is to drive or take a bus or join one of the many tours from Dresden. There is no train or tram service here. Driving is less than twenty minutes.

Website: www.Schloss-Moritzburg.de

Pillnitz Palace / Schloss Pillnitz: Located just a few miles upriver (East) on the Elbe from central Dresden, this absolutely huge facility can't help but impress. This is not just one big palace, it is a complex of buildings and formal gardens which covers almost 70 acres (28 hectares).

Pillnitz Palace / Schloss Pillnitz

Pillnitz Palace is a fully restored palace with elements of it dating back to the 14th century. It has been the residence of numerous area leaders including "electors" (think prince or senator as a comparable ranking) and even the home of a mistress of Augustus the Strong II's brother. (That must have been quite the relationship). It is an ornate Baroque-style complex with three main buildings, some of which are now museums. Adjacent to the array of buildings which line the river is a large parkland, much of which is formal open to visitors.

The Museums: Two museums are open here. The "Palace Museum" sits in the building known as the "New Palace" and tours are provided which include the chapel and tours of the kitchens. The other museum is the "Museum of Decorative Arts" a collection focused on Saxon and European art primarily from the 17th and 18th centuries.

Getting Here: If you are not driving your own car (a drive of less than 20 minutes), the best way to travel to here is to join one of the many tours from Dresden. Most of these

The Hop-On Bus does NOT come to here.

tours also include visits to other nearby palaces such as Moritzburg. Check the Dresden Tourist Office for details or simply do a web search for "Tours to Pillnitz from Dresden" and many options will be evident.

- By Boat: Consider doing this the fun way and taking a river cruise on a steamship from Dresden. Several firms such as www.GetYourGuide.com resell these boat trips.
- Travel by tram or bus: This is doable but a bit more complex and will likely require at least one change along the way. There is no tram stop close to this palace.

Website: Given the complexity of this property including multiple museums and expansive parkland, a visit to the website prior to your visit is suggested. www.SchlossPillnitz.de

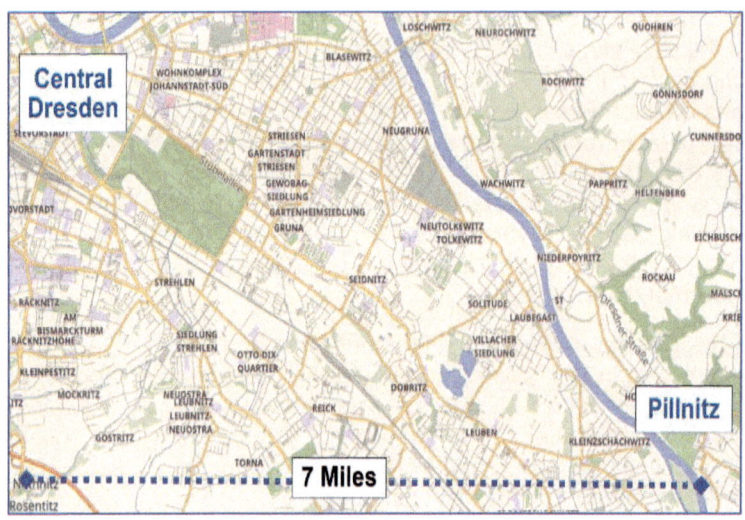

Saxon Switzerland National Park: To call this natural delight "a good day trip from Dresden" would be roughly akin to describing a fine Bordeaux wine as "a pleasant red liquid." If you enjoy natural rugged beauty, hiking through an incredibly varied set of trails, or enjoy exploring remote hilltop castles, then this is the destination for you. (This, of all locations outside of Dresden is the author's favorite). This natural wonder is only 30 kilometers east from central Dresden.

The Bastei Bridge in the Saxon Switerland National Park

You don't have to be athletic to enjoy the beauty here, but if you do have the ability to do some hiking, then you should strongly consider it. There is even a hiker's bus which takes you to popular trail points. This is one of the top day trip destinations out of Dresden and there is a lot to see for individuals of all abilities. One caution, the focal point, the Bastei Bridge, can be crowded.

In total, the park covers 270 square miles (700 square kilometers), but this is not contiguous. There are two major subsets to the park: (a) Germany – in the Elbe Sandstone Mountains; and (b) in the Czech Republic, with this section of the park known as the Bohemian Switzerland National Park. The German "Saxon Switzerland Park" accounts for 381 square kilometers of the park.

If you like hiking, there are over 740 miles (745 km) of marked trails. With this in mind, using an app such as All Trails or Komoot is suggested.

Königstein Fortress in Saxon Switerland National Park

Where to Start: Unless you have a specific section or trail in mind, head to the rock fortress Bastei. A bus-taxi combination to Bastei is available and takes about 90 minutes each way. Once you arrive at Bastei, there is about a ½ kilometer walk to the rock formations.

The Königstein Fortress/Festung: This hilltop fortress which overlooks the Elbe is just a few miles on foot and provides an attractive but arduous walk. If you wish to drive from Bastei to the fortress, this takes almost a half hour as there is no direct route. The fortress sits 790 feet above the river providing commanding views.

Tours: There are many tours to here from Dresden and most tours will be a full day. Look for tours to "Bohemian and Saxon Switzerland."

Website: Full details on this park, the trails, and transportation inside of the park may be found at: www.Saechsische-Schweiz.de. Guided tours of the park are available via this website.

Weesenstein Castle / Schloss Weesenstein: This imposing castle is in the small village of Müglitzal which is only 10 miles (16 km) southeast of Dresden. This location puts it roughly midway between Dresden and the Saxon Switzerland National Park.

Weesenstein Castle

The castle got its start around 1200 and was established as a fortress to defend the Kingdom of Bohemia. Major expansions were made in the 15th century and again in the 16th century with much of the updating shifting this to a palace instead of a fortress. During WWII, this was used as storage site for valuable art from surrounding museums.

Today, much of the castle and gardens are open to the public and is also a popular site for weddings and other events. To visit the castle, you must join a guided group tour and details are provided on their website.

Getting Here: Unfortunately, travel by public transportation is cumbersome and not advised. The best way to visit here is by car or join one of the tours from Dresden.

Website: www.Schloss-Weesenstein.de

Other Day Trip Locations: The seven destinations highlighted on the previous pages are far from all noteworthy sites to visit for day trips from Dresden. A few other locations to consider traveling to include:

- Grosssedlitz Barockgarten – Large palace and grounds often cited as "The Versailles of Saxony." Located a few miles southeast from Dresden. www.Barockgarten-Grosssedlitz.de

- Görlitz, Germany – Very appealing small town with numerous Gothic styled buildings. Just a few miles east from Dresden and easy to reach by train. www.Visit-Goerlitz.com

- Radebeul, Germany – Think wine. This area, which abuts Dresden's western suburbs, is known for its vineyards and wineries. www.Radebeul.de

- Chemnitz, Germany – An enjoyable small town to explore with tributes still in place to Karl Marx. www.Chemnitz.Travel

Note from the author: I hope you have found this guide to Dresden to be helpful in planning your visit. Comments and suggestions for improvement, or notes on any errors found, are always appreciated. Feel free to pass along any suggestions you may have to my email at cincy3@gmail.com

Appendix: Helpful Online References

To help you expand your knowledge of this area, several online reference sites are listed here. Dresden is a popular city to visit, so there is a wealth of material which can help in planning your trip.

The following is a list of online references about this city and area. The purpose of this list is to enhance your understanding of this area before embarking on your trip. Any online search will result in the websites outlined here plus many others. These are listed as they are professionally done and do not only try to sell you tours.

I.	Dresden City and Area Websites.
Website Name	**Website Address and Description**
Dresden City	www.Dresden.de Dresden City Website including the Tourist Office. Your best overall resource for services, tours, lodging, and attractions in Dresden.
City Card & Regio Card	www.Dresden.de Details on the city card and provisions to purchase the cards online in advance of your trip.
Dresden Football / Soccer	www.Dynamo-Dresden.de Learn about Dresden's professional soccer/football stadium and game schedule.

I.	Dresden City and Area Websites.
Website Name	**Website Address and Description**
Altmarkt-Galerie Shopping Center	Large shopping mall near Old Town – the Altmarkt-Galerie www.Altmrkt-Galerie-Dresden.de
Christmas Market	www.StriezelMarkt.Dresden.de Dresden has multiple Christmas markets. This site provides guidance on each of them.
Dresden Filmfest	www.Filmfest-Dresden.de Details and schedule for Dresden's popular annual film festival.
Dresden Music Festival	www.Musikfestspiele.com Find out about the annual music festival which occurs each May to June.
Schlosserland Card	Area discount card www.Schlosserland-Sachsen.de
You Tube	Several helpful videos available. One of the best is under the search term "Places to see in Dresden."
Wikipedia	www.Wikipedia.org OR simply do a search for Dresden Wikipedia and this site will appear on most search results pages. Detailed information on Dresden's history and the city's early development.

II. Dresden Museums and Attractions	
Museum / Attraction	Website
Frauenkirche Lutheran Church	www.Frauenkirche-Dresden.de
Dresden Cathedral	www.Bistum-Dresden-Meissen.de
Porcelain Museum	www.Porzellan-Museum.com
Dresden Xperience	Multi-media, immersive experience www.Festung-Xperience.com
Hygiene Museum	www.DHMD.de
Japanese Palace	Large complex with several museums. www.Japanisches-Palais.Skd.Museums
Military History Museum	The Bundeswehr Museum in Dresden's New Town. www.Mmmbw.de
Panometer Dresden	www.Panometer-Dresden.de
Pfunds Dairy Store	Popular, ornate dairy store. www.Pfunds.de
Porcelain Museum	www.Porzellan-Museum.com
Zoo – Dresden Zoo	www.Zoo-Dresden.de
Zwinger Museums	Several museums, including the Zwinger complex are covered with this website. www.SKD.Museum
Zwinger Xperience	Multi-media 360 experience. www.Zwinger-Xperience.com

III.	Area Castles, Towns, and Day Trips
Area	**Website Address and Description**
Bautzen, Germany	www.Bautzen.de
Leipzig, Germany	www.Leipzig.Travel
Meissen, Germany	www.Stadt-Meissen.de - Town www.Meissen.com – Porcelain www.Albrechtsburg-Meissen.de - Castle
Moritzburg Castle	www.Schloss-Moritzburg.de
Pillnitz Palace	www.SchlossPillnitz.de
Saxon Switzerland Park	www.Saechsische-Schweiz.de
Weesenstein Castle	www.Schloss-Weesenstein.de

IV.	Transportation Information and Tickets
Website Name	**Website Address & Description**
Airport Transportation	These services provide transportation from the Dresden airport plus other local taxi service • www.Taxi-Dresden.de • Dresdner Chauffer – www.8mal8.de • Taxi Schon– www.Taxi-Shuttle-ReiseService.de
Bicycle Rental	This firm is aligned with the DVB transportation network and also rents bikes in other cities. www.NextBike.de

Helpful Online Resources

IV.	Transportation Information and Tickets
Website Name	**Website Address & Description**
German Train System	www.Bahn.de Detailed travel schedules for Germany, rail passes, and ability to purchase train tickets.
Dresden Transportation & Funiculars	www.DVB.de This site covers local buses, trams, bike rentals, and the two funiculars.
Train Ticket Resellers	Several services enable you to purchase train tickets online prior to your trip, including: - RailEurope.com - Rome2rio.com - TrainLine.com - Eurorailways.com
Hop-On Bus Tours	www.Stadtrundfahrt.de

V.	Tour and Hotel Booking Sites
Company	**Website address and Description**
Hotel Sites	Numerous online sites enable you to review and book hotels online. Most of these sites also resell tours. - Booking.com - Hotels.com - Expedia.com - Travelocity.com

	V. Tour and Hotel Booking Sites
Company	**Website address and Description**
Tour Resellers	Many companies, such as the ones listed here, provide a full variety of tours to Dresden as well as day tours. - Dresden.de - GetYourGuide.com - ToursByLocals.com - Viator.com
Trip Advisor	www.TripAdvisor.com One of the most comprehensive sites on hotels and tours. Direct connection with Viator, a tour reseller.

Index

Airport Transportation 38
Albrechtsberg Palace............ 78
Altmarkt Plaza....................... 63
Altmarkt-Galerie 62
Apps to Download................ 11
Area Covered......................... 7
Attractions in Dresden.......... 40
Bautzen Daytrip 108
Bicycle Rentals 93
Brühl's Terrace 48
Bundeswehr Museum 76
Cable Cars........................... 80
Canaletto-Blick..................... 69
Castle Day Trips 107
Cathedral-Dresden 53
Christmas Market................. 33
City Passes.......................... 94
Climate Overview................. 28
Crown Gate - Zwinger.......... 57
Dairy Store - Pfunds............. 73
Day Trip Ideas 106
Dining Apps 12
Discount Cards 94
Dixieland Festival................. 32
Dresden Airport.................... 38
Dresden Castle 59
Dresden City Card 94
Dresden Xperience 50
Festivals and Events............ 31

Festung Dresden 50
Frauenkirche Church 46
Funiculars 80
Fürstenzug........................... 51
Golden Rider Statue 68
Grand Garden of Dresden ...85
Green Vault.......................... 60
Grosssedlitz Palace 124
Holy Cross Church............... 65
Hop-On Bus 88
Hotels in Dresden 99
Hygiene Museum 83
Introduction to Dresden........ 13
Itinerary Suggestions 8
Japanese Palace 70
King of Saxony Statue 68
Layout of Dresden 19
Leipzig Day Trip................. 111
Lodging Suggestions 99
Lutheran Church 65
Market Hall - Neustadt 72
Martin Luther Statue 45
Math Salon........................... 58
Meissen Day Trip............... 114
Military History Museum....... 76
Moritzburg Castle............... 117
Mountain Railway 81
Music Festival 32
National Park 121
Natural History Museum 70

Neumarkt Plaza....................44	Royal State Apartments 61
Neustadt Dresden 22	Saxon Switzerland Park 121
New Town Attractions 67	Schlosserland Card..............96
New Town Points of Interest 67	Science Instruments Msum..58
Old Masters Gallery..............57	Sculpture Museum 57
Old Town Dresden 42	Shopping Center 62
One Day Itinerary 8	Shopping Street 66
Palace Day Trips.................107	Soccer in Dresden................26
Palace of Culture..................64	Stallhof Dresden...................52
Palaces Near Dresden ...77, 78	Striezelmarkt 33
Panometer............................87	Subways & Trams 90
Park-Grosser Garden...........85	Suspension Railway 80
Pfunds Dairy Store 73	Tourist Office 10
Pillnitz Palace.....................118	Tours of Dresden..................97
Points of Interest List...........40	Train Stations in Dresden.....35
Porcelain Collection..............58	Trams in Dresden.................90
Prager Straße......................66	Transport Museum 45
Procession of Princes...........51	Travel Guidance...................34
Products Invented Here........27	Travel Planning Site 35
Public Transportation 90	Weesenstein Castle 123
Regio Disount Card..............94	WWII Notes 24
Rome2Rio App.....................35	Zoo.......................................86
Royal Palace 59	Zwinger Xperience 58

Starting-Point Travel Guides

www.StartingPointGuides.com

This guidebook on Dresden is one of several current and planned *Starting-Point Guides*. Each book in the series is developed with the concept of using one enjoyable city as your basecamp and then exploring from there.

Current guidebooks are for:

Austria:
- Salzburg, and the Salzburg area.

France:
- Bordeaux plus the surrounding Gironde River region
- Dijon plus the Burgundy Region
- Lille and the Nord-Pas-de-Calais Area.
- Lyon, Plus the Saône and Rhône Confluence Region
- Nantes and the western Loire Valley.
- Reims and Épernay the heart of the Champagne Region.
- Strasbourg and the central Alsace region.
- Toulouse and the Haute-Garonne area.

Germany:
- Cologne & Bonn
- Dresden and the Saxony State
- Stuttgart and the Baden-Württemberg area.

Spain:
- Camino Easy: A mature walker's guide to the popular Camino de Santiago trail.
- Toledo: The City of Three Cultures

Sweden:
- Gothenburg plus the Västra Götaland region.

Switzerland:
- Geneva including the Lake Geneva area.
- Lucerne including the Lake Lucerne area.
- Zurich – coming in mid-2024

Updates on these and other titles may be found on the author's Facebook page at: www.Facebook.com/BGPreston.author

Feel free to use this Facebook page to provide feedback and suggestions to the author or email to: cincy3@gmail.com

Printed in Great Britain
by Amazon